German

Visual Dictionary

for dummies®

WILEY

German Visual Dictionary For Dummies®

Published by
John Wiley & Sons, Inc.
111 River St.
Hoboken, NJ 07030-5774
www.wiley.com

Copyright © 2021 by John Wiley & Sons, Inc., Hoboken, New Jersey

No part of this publication may be reproduced, stored in a retrieval system or transmitted in any form or by any means, electronic, mechanical, photocopying, recording, scanning or otherwise, except as permitted under Sections 107 or 108 of the 1976 United States Copyright Act, without the prior written permission of the Publisher. Requests to the Publisher for permission should be addressed to the Permissions Department, John Wiley & Sons, Inc., 111 River Street, Hoboken, NJ 07030, (201) 748-6011, fax (201) 748-6008, or online at http://www.wiley.com/go/permissions.

Trademarks: Wiley, For Dummies, the Dummies Man logo, The Dummies Way, Dummies.com, Making Everything Easier, and related trade dress are trademarks or registered trademarks of John Wiley & Sons, Inc. and/or its affiliates in the United States and other countries, and may not be used without written permission. WQA and the WQA logo are trademarks or registered trademarks of the Water Quality Association. All other trademarks are the property of their respective owners. John Wiley & Sons, Inc., is not associated with any product or vendor mentioned in this book.

LIMIT OF LIABILITY/DISCLAIMER OF WARRANTY: THE PUBLISHER AND THE AUTHOR MAKE NO REPRESENTATIONS OR WARRANTIES WITH RESPECT TO THE ACCURACY OR COMPLETENESS OF THE CONTENTS OF THIS WORK AND SPECIFICALLY DISCLAIM ALL WARRANTIES, INCLUDING WITHOUT LIMITATION WARRANTIES OF FITNESS FOR A PARTICULAR PURPOSE. NO WARRANTY MAY BE CREATED OR EXTENDED BY SALES OR PROMOTIONAL MATERIALS. THE ADVICE AND STRATEGIES CONTAINED HEREIN MAY NOT BE SUITABLE FOR EVERY SITUATION. THIS WORK IS SOLD WITH THE UNDERSTANDING THAT THE PUBLISHER IS NOT ENGAGED IN RENDERING LEGAL, ACCOUNTING, OR OTHER PROFESSIONAL SERVICES. IF PROFESSIONAL ASSISTANCE IS REQUIRED, THE SERVICES OF A COMPETENT PROFESSIONAL PERSON SHOULD BE SOUGHT. NEITHER THE PUBLISHER NOR THE AUTHOR SHALL BE LIABLE FOR DAMAGES ARISING HEREFROM. THE FACT THAT AN ORGANIZATION OR WEBSITE IS REFERRED TO IN THIS WORK AS A CITATION AND/OR A POTENTIAL SOURCE OF FURTHER INFORMATION DOES NOT MEAN THAT THE AUTHOR OR THE PUBLISHER ENDORSES THE INFORMATION THE ORGANIZATION OR WEBSITE MAY PROVIDE OR RECOMMENDATIONS IT MAY MAKE. FURTHER, READERS SHOULD BE AWARE THAT INTERNET WEBSITES LISTED IN THIS WORK MAY HAVE CHANGED OR DISAPPEARED BETWEEN WHEN THIS WORK WAS WRITTEN AND WHEN IT IS READ.

For general information on our other products and services, or how to create a custom *For Dummies* book for your business or organization, please contact our Business Development Department in the U.S. at 877-409-4177, contact info@dummies.biz, or visit www.wiley.com/go/custompub. For information about licensing the *For Dummies* brand for products or services, contact BrandedRights&Licenses@Wiley.com.

Library of Congress Control Number: 2021933229

ISBN: 978-1-119-71714-0; ePDF: 978-1-119-71716-4; ePub: 978-1-119-71718-8

Table of Contents

Gute Nacht!
Good night! 95

Viel Spaß!
Let's go out! 111

Achtung!
Watch out! 157

Introduction

This *Visual Dictionary For Dummies* is your ideal travel companion. It can be carried conveniently and consulted quickly; all you have to do is show the picture of the thing you're talking about or of the situation you wish to describe, and presto! And since the pictures are accompanied by the corresponding English words and their German translations, you will also be able to learn a lot of new vocabulary!

Sounds, rhythm and intonation

German and English have a lot in common, including a common history. Both are *Indo-European* languages, meaning both made their way from the Indian subcontinent to Central Europe and beyond. (If you've ever wondered where the Saxon part of *Anglo-Saxon* came from, the Saxons were a Germanic tribe that made the move from Central Europe to the British Isles around the 5th Century A.D.) This common history means we share some vocabulary in common, and it also means that pronouncing German (for the most part) should be a breeze for English speakers.

The sounds: the vowels

Simple vowels

The vowels are divided into two groups: the so-called long or tense vowels and the so-called short or lax vowels.

- **kann (short a):** The German sound in **kann** is the sound you get if you go midway between **can** and **con**. If you are ever lucky enough to go to the Cannes Film Festival in France, you'll soon discover that the short "a" in **Cannes** sounds just like the German short "a."

- **Vater (long a):** The long "a" in German matches the short "a" in English, so **Vater** and **father** rhyme.
- **denn (short e):** To get the short German "e" sound, just think of the "e" sound in **when**.
- **eben (long e):** The German "e" sound in **eben** matches the sound we have for the "a" in **gate**.
- **im (short i):** The German sound **im** sounds exactly like the English sound in **sit**.
- **Igel (long i):** Think **eagle** when you want to say a long German "i" sound.
- **oft (short o):** The German sound **oft** is a good match for the short "o" sound in the English word **dog**.
- **Opa (long o):** Think **open** when you want to get the long German "o" sound. (Or just imagine you are in a Greek restaurant when they bring out the flaming cheese and you yell out **Opa!**)
- **um (short u):** The short "u" sound in German matches the vowel sound we have in the English word **wood**.
- **gut (long u):** The long "u" sound in German matches the vowel sound we have in the English word **boot**.

The "far from silent" e

Vase: Just keep in mind that there is no such thing as a silent "e" in German. If the "e" is there, you have to say it. That means **Vase** is a two-syllable word, with a long "a" in the first syllable and an *unaccented schwa* sound in the second syllable. ("Unaccented" here just means that you don't emphasize that syllable at all; the "schwa" sound is, believe it or not, the most common vowel sound in the English language.) For the second syllable (the schwa syllable), think of the sound in the word **uh** — that word we say when we are trying to think of a word — or the last syllable in a word like **banana**.

Umlauts

Here's where we venture into what might seem like strange territory: those two dots — known officially as umlauts — you see on vowels in the names of heavy metal bands and potent German alcoholic drinks. First and foremost, not all vowels can get the two dots — it's reserved for just "a's," "o's," and "u's." (That means if someone is putting the dots over an "i" and telling you it's a German word, they are pulling your leg.)

- **nächste (long ä):** The long "ä" in German has the sound of the "a" in the English word **hay**.
- **fällen (short ä):** The short "ä" in German has the sound of the "e" in the English word **bet**. Keep the sound short and clipped.
- **schön:** The "o" umlaut is close to the "er" sound in the English word **her**. Just don't stress the "r" sound. (So "schön" sounds very much like the made-up English word **shern** if you don't call too much attention to the "r.")
- **Tür:** The "u" umlaut sounds very much like the "u" in the English word **lure**. In fact, **Tür** and **lure** are a very good rhyme.

Diphthongs

As their name suggests, diphthongs are composed of two vowel sounds. German, like English, has a number of diphthongs — the words **Stein** and **Augen** come immediately to mind. As in English, the first vowel in German is strongly accented and slides into the second vowel. If you pay attention to how your mouth moves, you'll notice that it starts in one positon and ends up in another when pronouncing a diphthong.

- **Stein/Mais/Bayern:** All three spellings sound like the "y" in the English word **cry**.
- **Laut:** The German "au" diphthong sounds like the "ou" in the English word **loud**.

7

- **Häuser/Leute:** Both spellings here sound like the "oy" sound in the English word **boy**.

In American English, there's no hard and fast rule about how to pronounce "ei" versus "ie." Just think of the famous American composer Leonard Bernstein. Half his audience called him "Leonard Bernsteen" and the other half call him "Leonard Bernstine." In German, the "ie" sound is always the "e" sound in **see** and the "ei" sound is always the sound of **aye**, as in **aye, aye, captain**. Just remember that "ie" ends with an "e," so you have to say "e," whereas "ei" ends with an "i," so you have to say "i."

The sounds: the consonants

Most German consonants match the sound of English consonants exactly, but you'll need to pay particular attention to some that are tricky for English speakers to pronounce.

- **"th":** Most of the time, Germans don't like the idea of silent letters. There's no such thing as a silent "e," for example, and they are completely thrown off by English words like **weight** and **doubt**. The rule is usually "if you see it, say it." The one exception is the "th" sound. Here, the "h" is silent. That means a word like **Theater** starts with the same "t" sound you would hear in the English word **table**.
- **"kn":** Continuing with the theme of "if you see it, say it," Germans always pronounce the "k" sound in the combination "kn." That means that although the English word **knee** is pronounced "nee," the German word **Knie** is pronounced "kuh-nee," said very quickly.
- **"ps":** One final "if you see it, say it" example is the "ps" sound. Germans insist that you sneak in a "p" sound before the "s." That means the English word **psychology** (pronounced "sigh-cology") is quite different from the German word

Psychologie, which is more like "psssuuu-cology." (The English word "psssssst!!" is the closest we have to this German sound.)

- **"b":** When a German "b" is at the beginning or middle of the word, it matches the English "b" sound. When it ends a word or comes before an "s," however, it has the English "p" sound. That means **Dieb** sounds exactly like **deep** and **lebst** rhymes with the English word **cape** with an "st" added at the end.

- **"d":** When a German "d" is at the beginning or middle of a word, it matches the English "d" sound. When it ends a word or is used in combination with an "s" (**Bands**) or "t" (**Stadt**), it has the "t" sound. That means the German word **Tod** sounds like the English word **tote**, as in a **tote bag**.

- **"g":** When a German "g" is used at the beginning or middle of a word, it always has the soft "g" sound of the English word **gone** and never the hard "g" sound of the word "giraffe." When used at the end of the word, it has a "k" sound. That means **Tag** sounds more like the **tock** in **tick tock**.

- **"ch":** When used at the beginning of a word, the German "ch" matches the "ch" used in an English word like **character** — in other words, it sounds like a "k." When used in the middle of a word and preceded by a, o, u, or au (**Bücher**), it sounds more like the "sh" heard in the English word "cashier." Finally, when used at the end of a word, it has the sound the Scots would use to speak of the **Loch Ness Monster**.

- **"r":** When used at the beginning of a word, Germans "roll their r's," which is something English speakers rarely do. The closest we come is when we try to imitate a dog by saying **rrrrruuuufff rrrrrrruuuuffff!** That means the "r" in the German word "rot" is more like the "r" in **rrrrrrrrro rrrrrrrro rrrrrrrrosey, goodbye**.

- **"v":** The German "v," when used at the beginning of a word, sounds exactly like the English "f." That means **viel** sounds like the English word **feel**. When "v" is in the middle or at the end of a word, it sounds like what you'd expect a "v" to sound like. That means **privat** sounds like **private** as far as the "v" is concerned.
- **"w":** The German "w" sounds exactly like the English "v" no matter where the "w" shows up. That means a phrase like **wie viel** (which means "how much?") sounds like "vee feel" in English.
- **"z":** The German "z" sounds more like a "ts," which is a rare sound in English at the beginning of a word — except for exotic creatures like **tsetse flies**. It is a common sound in the middle of English words, however. In fact, if you can say **pizza**, you can say the German "z."

Unterwegs!

Let's go!

Das Flugzeug
The airplane

der Flughafen
the airport

das Flugzeug
the airplane

die Fluggesellschaft
the airline

der Schalter
the ticket counter

das Gepäck
the baggage

das Handgepäck
the carry-on luggage

die Reisetasche
the travel bag

der Koffer
the suitcase

der Gepäckwagen
the luggage cart

die Flüssigkeiten
the liquids

das Sicherheitsportal
the security gate

der Personalausweis
the identification card

Das Flugzeug
The airplane

**der Reisepass/
der Pass**
the passport

die Reiseabfertigung
the check-in

der Zoll
customs

das Flugticket
the plane ticket

das Rückflugticket
the return flight ticket

der Flugsteig
the airport gate

die Bordkarte
the boarding pass

das Einchecken
the boarding

der Notausgang
the emergency exit

der Flugkapitän
the flight captain

der Flug
the flight

am Fenster
at the window

13

Das Flugzeug
The airplane

am Gang
in the aisle

der Sicherheitsgurt
the seat belt

die Schwimmweste
the life jacket

die Sauerstoffmaske
the oxygen mask

der Abflug
the departure

die Ankunft
the arrival

das Gepäckband
the baggage carousel

der Shuttlebus
the shuttle bus

Das Flugzeug
The airplane

Schlüsselsätze	Key phrases
Wo ist der . . . Schalter?	Where is the . . . counter?
Ich möchte mein Ticket abholen.	I want to pick up my ticket.
Wann muss ich einchecken?	When do I have to check in?
Können Sie sich ausweisen?	Do you have identification?
Haben Sie Gepäck?	Do you have luggage?
Wie viele Gepäckstücke kann ich mitnehmen?	How many pieces of luggage can I take?
Wie lange dauert der Flug?	How long is the flight?
Wann fliegt die Maschine ab?	When does the plane take off?
Wo möchten Sie sitzen, am Fenster oder am Gang?	Where would you like to sit, at the window or the aisle?
Ich bin im Urlaub hier.	I'm here on vacation.
Ich bin auf der Durchreise nach . . .	I'm on my way to . . .
Wann kommt die Maschine aus . . . an?	When does the plane from . . . arrive?
Das Flugzeug ist pünktlich um dreizehn Uhr gelandet.	The plane landed on time at 1 PM.

Zug und öffentlicher Nahverkehr
Trains and public transport

der Bahnhof
the train station

der Bahnsteig
the platform

das Gleis
the track

der Zug
the train

die Fahrkarte
the train ticket

das Ticket
the ticket

die erste Klasse
first class

die zweite Klasse
second class

der Sitzplatz
the seat

die Auskunft
information

die Rückfahrkarte
the return ticket

die Platzkarte
the seat reservation

Zug und öffentlicher Nahverkehr
Trains and public transport

die Abfahrt
the departure

die Verspätung
the delay

der Fahrplan
the schedule

einsteigen
get on the train

aussteigen
get off the train

die Ankunft
the arrival

die Schlange
the line

die Fahrkarte
the ticket

der Fahrkartenschalter
the ticket counter

der Fahrkartenautomat
the ticket machine

der Bus
the bus

der Busfahrer
the bus driver

Zug und öffentlicher Nahverkehr

Trains and public transport

die U-Bahn
the subway

die S-Bahn
the commuter train

die Straßenbahn
the streetcar

die Bushaltestelle
the bus stop

die U-Bahnlinie
the subway line

die U-Bahnstation
the subway station

die Haltestelle
the station

die Seilbahn
the cable car

Zug und öffentlicher Nahverkehr

Trains and public transport

Schlüsselsätze	Key phrases
Eine Fahrkarte nach . . . , bitte.	A ticket to . . . please.
Einfach oder hin und zurück?	One-way or a return ticket?
Was kostet eine einfache Fahrt nach . . . ?	How much is a one-way ticket to . . . ?
Von welchem Gleis fährt der Zug nach . . . ab?	From which track is the train to . . . departing?
Auf welchem Gleis kommt der Zug aus . . . an?	On which track is the train from . . . arriving?
Hat der Zug Verspätung?	Is the train delayed?
Gibt es einen direkten Zug von . . . nach . . . ?	Is there a direct train from . . . to . . . ?
Nein, Sie müssen in . . . umsteigen.	No, you have to change trains in . . .
Welche Buslinie fährt ins Stadtzentrum?	Which bus line goes to the city center?
Ist das die richtige Straßenbahn zum Stadion?	Is this the right streetcar to the stadium?
Muß ich umsteigen?	Do I have to transfer?
Hält diese U-Bahn am Hauptbahnhof?	Does this subway stop at the central station?

Der Wagen
The car

der Wagen
the car

der Führerschein
the driver's license

der Airbag
the Airbag®

der Sicherheitsgurt
the seat belt

das Rad
the wheel

die Bremse
the brake

der Rückspiegel
the rearview mirror

das Lenkrad
the steering wheel

das Armaturenbrett
the dashboard

der Motor
the motor

der Kofferraum
the trunk

der Scheinwerfer
the headlight

Der Wagen
The car

der Tank
the tank

das Nummernschild
the license plate

die Scheibenwischer
the windshield wipers

die Landstraße
the country road

die Ampel
the traffic light

die Straßenkarte
the street map

die Autobahn
the highway

die Ausfahrt
the on-ramp

die Auffahrt
the off-ramp

das Autobahnkreuz
the highway intersection

die Notrufsäule
the emergency call station

der Parkplatz
the parking lot

Der Wagen
The car

Parken verboten
parking prohibited

Einbahnstraße
one-way street

Durchfahrt verboten
no entry

Licht an/aus
lights on/off

Umleitung
detour

Vorsicht Glatteis
caution, icy road

Baustelle
construction site

der Tunnel
the tunnel

der Unfall
the accident

der Abschleppwagen
the tow truck

der Verkehr
the traffic

Der Wagen
The car

Schlüsselsätze	Key phrases
Gibt es hier irgendwo eine Werkstatt?	Is there a repair shop nearby?
Wo finde ich eine Tankstelle?	Where can I find a gas station?
Ich habe eine Panne.	My car broke down.
Wir steckten in einem Verkehrsstau.	We were in a traffic jam.

Die Autovermietung
The car rental office

die Autovermietung
the car rental office

der Führerschein
the driver's license

**ein zweitüriges/
viertüriges Auto**
a two-door/four-door car

die Limousine
the sedan

der Kombi
the station wagon

der Van
the van

das Kabriolett
the convertible

das Coupé
the coupe

mieten
to rent

fahren
to drive

der Schaden
the damage

das Problem
the problem

24

Die Autovermietung
The car rental office

Schlüsselsätze	Key phrases
Für wie lange möchten Sie den Wagen mieten?	For how long do you want to rent the car?
Ab wann möchten Sie den Wagen mieten?	From when do you want to rent the car?
Wann/wo möchten Sie den Wagen zurückgeben?	When/where do you want to return the car?
Ich möchte den Wagen ab dem . . . mieten.	I want to rent the car from . . .
Ich möchte den Wagen bis zum . . . mieten.	I want to rent the car until . . .
Ich möchte den Wagen am . . . zurückgeben.	I want to return the car on . . .
Ich möchte den Wagen in . . . zurückgeben.	I want to return the car in . . .

Das Taxi
The taxi

| **das Taxi** | **der Taxistand** | **der Taxifahrer** |
| the taxi | the taxi stand | the taxi driver |

Schlüsselsätze	**Key phrases**
Können Sie mir bitte ein Taxi bestellen?	Could you please call a taxi for me?
Wo ist der nächste Taxistand?	Where is the nearest taxi stand?
Sind Sie frei?	Are you free?
Wohin möchten Sie?	Where do you want to go?
Bitte zum Flughafen.	To the airport, please.
Wie viel kostet eine Fahrt zum Bahnhof?	How much is a ride to the train station?
Ich hätte gern ein Taxi nach/ zum/zur . . .	I would like a taxi to . . .
Bitte bringen Sie mich zu dieser Adresse.	Please bring me to this address.
Sie können hier anhalten, vielen Dank.	You can stop here, thank you.

Das Fahrrad
The bicycle

das Fahrrad
the bicycle

der Helm
the helmet

der Sattel
the saddle

der Lenker
the handlebar

die Bremse
the brake

das Pedal
the pedal

die Kette
the chain

der Reifen
the tire

die Felge
the rim

die Klingel
the bell

das Flickzeug
the repair kit

die Luftpumpe
the air pump

27

Das Fahrrad
The bicycle

der Fahrradweg
the bike path

das Fahrradschloss
the bicycle lock

die Wasserflasche
the water bottle

der Fahrradstand
the bike rack

die Sicherheitsweste
the safety vest

Schlüsselsätze	Key phrases
Ich suche ein Fahrradgeschäft.	I'm looking for a bicycle shop.
Ich möchte für einen Tag ein Fahrrad leihen.	I want to rent a bicycle for a day.
Wie weit ist es?	How far is it?
Haben Sie eine Radwanderkarte?	Do you have a cycling map?
Können Sie es mir auf der Karte zeigen?	Can you show me on the map?

Hallo!

Hello!

Sich begrüßen und sich verabschieden
Saying hello and goodbye

Hallo!
Hello!

Grüß dich!
Hello there!

Guten Morgen!
Good morning! (the morning)

Wie geht's?
How are you?

Guten Nachmittag!
Good Afternoon

Guten Abend!
Good evening! (after 6 PM)

der Händedruck
the handshake

sich küssen
kissing one another

Sich begrüßen und sich verabschieden
Saying hello and goodbye

Schlüsselsätze	Key phrases
Wie geht's?	How are you?
Danke, gut.	Fine, thanks.
Sehr gut.	Very well.
Nicht so gut.	Not so well.
Und Ihnen?	And you? (formal)
Und dir?	And you? (informal)
Freut mich, Sie kennenzulernen.	I'm pleased to meet you.
Meinerseits. / Ganz meinerseits.	Likewise.
Ich heiße . . .	My name is . . .
Ich komme aus Deutschland.	I come from Germany.
Wir duzen uns.	Let's be informal with one another.
Wir siezen uns.	Let's keep it formal.

Höflich Fragen stellen, sich bedanken und sich entschuldigen
Politely asking questions, saying thanks and apologizing

**Entschuldigen
Sie bitte.**
Please excuse me.

**Entschuldigen Sie,
bitte!**
Excuse me, please!

Bitte!
Please!

Danke, das war gut.
Thank you, that was good.

Sehr gut.
Very good.

Ausgezeichnet!
Excellent!

Das tut mir leid.
I'm sorry.

Entschuldigung.
Sorry!

Sich verabschieden
Saying goodbye

Tschüss!
Bye!

Auf Wiedersehen!
Goodbye!

Gute Nacht!
Good night!

Bis morgen!
See you tomorrow!

Bis später!
See you later!

Bis bald!
See you soon!

Gute Reise!
Have a nice trip!

Sich verabschieden
Saying goodbye

Schlüsselsätze	Key phrases
War nett, Sie kennenzulernen.	It was nice to meet you.
Bleiben wir in Kontakt?	Should we stay in touch?
Haben Sie eine E-Mail-Adresse?	Do you have an email address?
Haben Sie ein Facebook-Konto?	Are you on Facebook?

Die Zeit
The time

pünktlich
punctual

zu früh
too early

verspätet
late

die Uhrzeit
the time of day

die Stunde
the hour

die Minute
the minute

das Viertel
the quarter (hour)

halb
half (hour)

der Morgen
the morning

der Mittag
noon

der Nachmittag
the afternoon

der Abend
the evening

Die Zeit
The time

tagsüber
during the day

die Nacht
the night

heute Abend
tonight

Schlüsselsätze	Key phrases
Morgen Abend.	Tomorrow evening.
Heute Mittag.	Noon today.
Morgen Mittag.	Noon tomorrow.
Entschuldigen Sie, bitte, wie viel Uhr ist es?	Excuse me, what time is it?
Wie spät ist es?	What time is it?
Es ist zehn Uhr.	It's ten o'clock.
Es ist Viertel nach drei.	It's three fifteen.
Es ist Viertel vor zwölf.	It's a quarter to twelve.

Sich orientieren

Orienting yourself

Sich zurechtfinden
Finding your way around

das Fremdenverkehrsbüro
the tourist office

die Landkarte
the map

der Stadtplan
the city map

das (Stadt-)Zentrum
the (city) center

die Fußgängerzone
the pedestrian zone

der Stadtteil
the district

die Straße
the street

die Kreuzung
the intersection

der Kreisverkehr
the roundabout

der Fußgängerübergang
the crosswalk

der Bürgersteig
the sidewalk

der Platz
the square

Sich zurechtfinden
Finding your way around

das Gebäude
the building

der Fluss
the river

der Hafen
the port

die Brücke
the bridge

der Parkplatz
the parking lot

der Markt
the market

das Rathaus
the city hall

der Bahnhof
the train station

das Stadion
the stadium

der Flughafen
the airport

das Krankenhaus
the hospital

die Apotheke
the pharmacy

Sich zurechtfinden
Finding your way around

die Bank
the bank

die Post
the post office

der Supermarkt
the supermarket

Schlüsselsätze	Key phrases
Hätten Sie einen Stadtplan?	Do you have a city map?
Gibt es eine Städtführung?	Is there a city tour?
Haben Sie Informationen zu den örtlichen Sehenswürdigkeiten?	Do you have any information about the local attractions?
Ich möchte . . . besichtigen.	I want to visit . . .

Nach dem Weg fragen
Asking for directions

abbiegen
turn

folgen
follow

geradeaus
straight ahead

hinaufgehen
go up

hinuntergehen
go down

links
left

rechts
right

umkehren
turn around

weitergehen
continue

41

Nach dem Weg fragen
Asking for directions

N
der Norden
the north

E
der Osten
the east

S
der Süden
the south

W
der Westen
the west

links von
to the left of

rechts von
to the right of

vor
in front of

hinter
behind

hier
here

Nach dem Weg fragen
Asking for directions

Schlüsselsätze	Key phrases
Wie kommt man da hin?	How do you get there?
Können Sie mir das auf dem Plan zeigen?	Can you show me on a map?
Bin ich hier richtig auf dem Weg nach/zu . . . ?	Is this the right way to . . . ?

Sehenswürdigkeiten in der Stadt

Attractions in the city

die Altstadt
the historic district

der Park
the park

der Brunnen
the fountain

die Statue
the statue

der Kiosk
the kiosk

der Flohmarkt
the flea market

die Bibliothek
the library

das Theater
the theater

die Oper
the opera

der Dom
the cathedral

die Kirche
the church

das Kloster
the monastery

Sehenswürdigkeiten in der Stadt

Attractions in the city

die Moschee
the mosque

die Synagoge
the synagogue

die Abtei
the abbey

die Burg
the castle

die Festung
the fortress

die Ruine
the ruin

der See
the lake

die Stadtmauer
the city wall

der Wolkenkratzer
the skyscrapers

der Zoo
the zoo

das Restaurant
the restaurant

das Café
the café

Sehenswürdigkeiten in der Stadt
Attractions in the city

das Hotel
the hotel

das Geschäft
the shop

Schlüsselsätze	Key phrases
Ich hätte gern eine Auskunft über . . .	I would like information about . . .
Wo ist die Burg?	Where is the castle?
Wo sollen wir uns treffen?	Where should we meet?
Der Dom liegt an der Straßenecke.	The cathedral is at the street corner.
Ist es kostenlos?	Is it free?

Öffentliche Toiletten
Public toilets

Toiletten (Damen)
toilets (women)

Toiletten (Herren)
toilets (men)

gebührenpflichtig
charges apply

kostenlos
free

behindert
handicapped

der Wickeltisch
the diaper changing station

die Seife
the soap

das Toilettenpapier
the toilet paper

der Händetrockner
the hair dryer

Schlüsselsätze

Key phrases

Entschuldigen Sie, bitte, wo sind die Toiletten?

Excuse me, please, where are the toilets?

Das Wetter
The weather

das Wetter
the weather

die Wettervorhersage
the weather forecast

warm
warm

kalt
cold

die Sonne
the sun

sonnig
sunny

der Wind
the wind

der Sturm
the storm

bewölkt
cloudy

die Temperatur
the temperature

regnerisch
rainy

feucht
humid

Das Wetter
The weather

windig
windy

kühl
cool

der Frost
the frost

der Schnee
the snow

Schlüsselsätze	Key phrases
Es ist schön.	It's beautiful.
Die Sonne scheint.	The sun is shining.
Es ist kalt.	It's cold.
Es ist heiß.	It's hot.
Es wird regnen.	It's going to rain.
Was für ein herrliches Wetter!	The weather is great!
Was für ein schreckliches Wetter!	The weather is terrible!

Verschiedene Landschaften
Different landscapes

das Land
the country

der Wald
the forest

das Feld
the field

der Baum
the tree

die Wiese
the meadow

der Berg
the mountain

das Gebirge
the mountains

der Hügel
the hill

das Tal
the valley

der Fluss
the river

der See
the lake

der Wasserfall
the waterfall

Verschiedene Landschaften
Different landscapes

der Ozean
the ocean

die See
the sea

die Küste
the coast

der Bodensee
Lake Constance

Schlüsselsätze	Key phrases
Wir haben den Bodensee gesehen.	We saw Lake Constance.
Sie hat die Ostsee gesehen.	She saw the Baltic Sea.
Ich habe einen Vogel beobachtet.	I watched a bird.
Ich habe einen See gesehen.	I saw a lake.

Orientierungspunkte
Landmarks

das Naturschutzgebiet
the nature reserve

die Gegend
the area

spazieren gehen
going for a walk

die Wanderung
the hike

die Karte
the map

der Weg
the path

der Bauernhof
the farm

die Brücke
the bridge

der Fluss
the river

der Bach
the creek

das Dorf
the village

die Kirche
the church

Orientierungspunkte
Landmarks

die Mühle
the mill

die Berghütte
the mountain cabin

die Hütte
the hut

die Seilbahn
the cable car

Schlüsselsätze	Key phrases
Wir fahren in die Berge.	We're going to the mountains.
Wir fahren aufs Land.	We're going to the countryside.
Wir machen Urlaub auf dem Bauernhof.	We're taking a vacation on a farm.
Ich gehe im Wald spazieren.	I'm walking in the forest.

Guten Appetit!

Enjoy your meal!

Geschirr und Besteck
Kitchenware and cutlery

das Glas
the glass

die Tasse
the cup

der Teller
the plate

der Suppenteller
the soup plate

die Serviette
the napkin

das Messer
the knife

die Gabel
the fork

der Löffel
the spoon

das Besteck
the cutlery

Mahlzeiten und Gerichte
Meals and dishes

das Frühstück
the breakfast

das Mittagessen
the lunch

Kaffee und Kuchen
coffee and cake

das Abendessen
the dinner

der Aperitif
the apéritif

die Vorspeisen
the appetizers

das Hauptgericht
the main course

die Nachspeise
the dessert

Imbiss
snack

Schlüsselsätze	Key phrases

Ich habe Hunger.	I'm hungry.
Ich bin durstig.	I'm thirsty.
Gehen wir etwas essen?	Do you want to go out to eat?

Das Frühstück
The breakfast

das Brot
the bread

das Brötchen
the bread roll

das Weißbrot
the white bread

das Schwarzbrot
the rye bread

der Toast
the toast

der Aufschnitt
the cold cuts

die Butter
the butter

die Konfitüre
the jam

die Kornflakes
the corn flakes

das Müsli
the granola

die Milch
the milk

der Kaffee
the coffee

Das Frühstück
The breakfast

der Tee
the tea

die Schokolade
the hot chocolate

der Zucker
the sugar

der Honig
the honey

der Saft
the juice

die Wurst
the sausage

das Ei
the egg

das Spiegelei
the sunny-side-up egg

die Rühreier
the scrambled eggs

der Käse
the cheese

der Joghurt
the yogurt

das Croissant
the croissant

Das Frühstück
The breakfast

das Baguette
the baguette

Schlüsselsätze	Key phrases
Was nehmen Sie?	What will you have?
Ich nehme einen Tee.	I'll have some tea.
Einen Kaffee, bitte.	A coffee, please.

Fleisch, Fisch und Meeresfrüchte

Meat, fish and seafood

das Kotelett
the cutlet

die Bratwurst
the bratwurst

das Rindfleisch
the beef

der Rinderbraten
the roast beef

das Beefsteak
the steak

das Hackfleisch
hamburger meat

das Kalbfleisch
the veal

das Schweinefleisch
the pork

das Lamm
the lamb

die Wurst
the sausage

die Ente
the duck

das Hähnchen
the chicken

Fleisch, Fisch und Meeresfrüchte
Meat, fish and seafood

das Kaninchen
the rabbit

die Leber
the liver

der Schinken
the ham

der Speck
the bacon

die Pastete
the paté

der Fisch
the fish

der Kabeljau
the cod

der Thunfisch
the tuna

der Seebarsch
the sea bass

die Sardinen
the sardines

die Makrele
the mackerel

der Wittling
the whiting

Fleisch, Fisch und Meeresfrüchte
Meat, fish and seafood

der Lachs
the salmon

die Rotbarbe
the red mullet

die Sardelle
the anchovy

der Hering
the herring

der Hecht
the pike

die Seezunge
the sole

die Forelle
the trout

der Seeteufel
the monkfish

die Meeresfrüchte
the seafood

die Garnele
the shrimp

die Nordseegarnele
the brown shrimp

die Muschel
the mussel

Fleisch, Fisch und Meeresfrüchte
Meat, fish and seafood

die Auster
the oyster

die Jakobsmuschel
the scallop

die Krabbe
the crab

der Hummer
the lobster

die Languste
the crawfish

der Krebs
the prawn

Das Gemüse
The vegetables

das Gemüse
the vegetables

die Karotte
the carrot

der Salat
the salad

die Linsen
the lentils

die Bohne
the bean

die Butterbohnen
the butter beans

der Brokkoli
the broccoli

die Erbse
the pea

die Gurke
the cucumber

die Kartoffel
the potato

der Kopfsalat
the lettuce

der Porree
the leek

Das Gemüse
The vegetables

der Paprika
the bell pepper

der Pilz
the mushroom

der Kohl
the cabbage

das Sauerkraut
the sauerkraut

der Rosenkohl
the Brussels sprouts

der Spinat
the spinach

die Tomate
the tomato

die Zucchini
the zucchini

das Radieschen
the radish

die rote Beete
the beet

die Artischocke
the artichoke

die Aubergine
the eggplant

Das Gemüse
The vegetables

die Avocado
the avocado

der Fenchel
the fennel

Reis, Nudeln und Beilagen
Rice, noodles and side dishes

der Reis
the rice

die Kartoffel
the potato

die Nudeln
the noodles

die Bohne
the beans

die weißen Bohnen
the white beans

die grünen Bohnen
the green beans

die grünen Linsen
the green lentils

der Weizengrieß
the semolina

der Mais
the corn

Die Nachspeise
The desserts

die Nachspeise
the dessert

das Obst
the fruit

der Obstsalat
the fruit salad

der Kuchen
the cake

der Apfelstrudel
the apple strudel

die Torte
the tart

Das Apfelmus
Applesauce

das Eis
the ice cream

die Schlagsahne
the whipped cream

die Waffel
the waffle

die Crêpe
the crepe

die Brioche
the brioche

69

Die Nachspeise
The desserts

der Schokoladeeisbecher
the chocolate sundae

das Mousse au chocolat
the chocolate mousse

der Keks
the cookie

Obst
Fruit

das Obst
the fruit

der Apfel
the apple

die Banane
the banana

die Birne
the pear

die Orange
the orange

die Clementine
the clementine

die Grapefruit
the grapefruit

die Zitrone
the lemon

die Weintraube
the grape

die Erdbeere
the strawberry

die Pflaume
the plum

die Feige
the fig

Obst
Fruit

die Kirsche
the cherry

der Pfirsich
the peach

die Aprikoses
the apricot

die Kiwi
the kiwi

die Ananas
the pineapple

die Limone
the lime

die rote Johannisbeeres
the red currant

die Brombeere
the blackberry

die Himbeere
the raspberry

die Heidelbeere
the blueberry

die schwarze Johannisbeere
the black currant

die Melone
the melon

Obst
Fruit

die Wassermelone
the watermelon

die Mango
the mango

die Rosinen
the raisins

Gewürze
Seasonings

das Salz
the salt

der Pfeffer
the pepper

das Öl
the oil

das Olivenöl
the olive oil

der Essig
the vinegar

der Senf
the mustard

die Mayonnaise
the mayonnaise

der Ketchup
the ketchup

die Peperoni
the chili

die Nelken
the cloves

die Lorbeerblätter
the bay leaves

die Muskatnuss
the nutmeg

Gewürze
Seasonings

der Zimt
the cinnamon

der Kümmel
the caraway seed

der Paprika
the paprika

der Safran
the saffron

der Ingwer
the ginger

der Kardamom
the cardamom

die Zwiebel
the onion

der Knoblauch
the garlic

die Schalotte
the shallot

die Petersilie
the parsley

der Thymian
the thyme

der Rosmarin
the rosemary

Gewürze
Seasonings

der Lorbeer
the laurel

der Schnittlauch
the chive

der Kerbel
the chervil

der Dill
the dill

der Koriander
the coriander

der Oregano
the oregano

der Meerrettich
the horseradish

der Estragon
the tarragon

die Minze
the mint

das Basilikum
the basil

der Salbei
the sage

Gewürze
Seasonings

Schlüsselsätze	Key phrases
Es ist überwürzt.	It's too spicy.
Es fehlt Salz.	It needs salt.

Restaurants und Gaststätten
Restaurants and taverns

das Restaurant
the restaurant

die Gaststätte
the tavern

der Gasthofs
the inn

der Rasthof
the rest stop service area

die Bierstube
the beer hall

die Weinstube
the wine bar

die Kneipe
the pub

das Café
the café

**der Imbiss/
Schnellimbiss**
the snack bar/fast-food stand

Restaurants und Gaststätten
Restaurants and taverns

Schlüsselsätze	Key phrases
Entschuldigen Sie, bitte!	Excuse me, please!
Kann ich bitte einen Löffel/eine Gabel/ein Messer haben?	May I please get a spoon/fork/knife?
Dürfen wir rauchen?	May we smoke?

Die Reservierung
The reservation

die Reservierung
the reservation

die Speisekarte
the menu

die Weinkarte
the wine list

der Kellner
the waiter

ein freier Tisch
a free table

zum Mitnehmen
to go

zum sofortigen Verzehr
to eat now

Raucher
smoking

Nichtraucher
non-smoking

Die Reservierung
The reservation

Schlüsselsätze	Key phrases
Ich möchte gern einen Tisch reservieren/ bestellen.	I would like to reserve/ order a table.
Haben Sie um . . . Uhr einen Tisch frei?	Do you have a free table at . . . o'clock?
Ich möchte gern einen Tisch für . . . Personen um . . . Uhr reservieren.	I would like to reserve a table for . . . people at . . . o'clock.
In . . . Minuten wird ein Tisch frei.	A table will be free in . . . minutes.
Können Sie in . . . Minuten wiederkommen?	Can you come back in . . . minutes?
Ich möchte gern für heute Abend einen Tisch reservieren.	I would like to reserve a table for this evening.
Haben Sie morgen Mittag um . . . Uhr einen Tisch frei ?	Do you have a free table for lunch tomorrow at . . . o'clock?

Einige Gerichte
A few dishes

die Suppe
the soup

der Salat
the salad

Melone mit Schinken
melon and ham

Meerfrüchtesalat mit Toastecken
seafood salad with toast

Gurkensalat
cucumber salad

das belegte Brot
the sandwich

die Pizza
the pizza

der Hamburger
the hamburger

die Pommes frites
the French fries

die Chips
the chips

die Bratkartoffeln
the fried potatoes

das Knoblauchbrot
the garlic bread

Einige Gerichte
A few dishes

Schlüsselsätze	Key phrases
Ich hätte gern . . .	I would like . . .
Für mich bitte . . .	For me, please, . . .
Ich möchte gern . . .	I would like to . . .
Ich würde gern . . . essen/haben.	I would like to eat/have . . .

Regionale Spezialitäten
Regional specialties

das Sauerkraut
the sauerkraut

der Kartoffelsalat
the potato salad

die Currywurst
the currywurst

die Kartoffelknödel
the potato dumplings

die Spätzle
the spaetzle

das Eisbein
the pork knuckle

die Brezel
the pretzel

der Kebab
the kebab

der Schweinebraten
the roast pork

die Schwarzwälder Kirschtorte
the Black Forest cake

der Apfelstrudel
the apple strudel

der Käsekuchen
the cheesecake

Regionale Spezialitäten
Regional specialties

die Plätzchen
the cookies

der Stollen
the Christmas fruit cake

das Vollkornbrot
the whole-grain bread

der Berliner
the jelly-filled doughnut

der Bienenstich
the "bee sting" cake with almonds

die rote Grütze
the red fruit jelly

Schlüsselsätze	Key phrases
Können Sie etwas empfehlen?	Can you recommend anything?
Hat es Ihnen geschmeckt?	How did things taste?
Danke, gut.	Thank you, it tasted good.
Sehr gut.	Very good.
Ausgezeichnet.	Excellent!

Gerichte für Allergiker, Vegetarier und Kindermenus
Meals for people with allergies, vegetarians and children

vegetarische Gerichte
vegetarian dishes

Ich kann nichts essen, was... enthält.
I can't eat anything that contains...

Gerichte für Diabetiker
meals for diabetics

Kinderportionen
children's portions

allergisch gegen...
allergic to...

ohne Soße
without sauce

ohne Salz
without salt

zuckerfrei
without sugar

ohne Gluten
without gluten

Gerichte für Allergiker, Vegetarier und Kindermenus

Meals for people with allergies, vegetarians and children

Schlüsselsätze	Key phrases
Haben Sie vegetarische Gerichte?	Do you have vegetarian dishes?
Ich kann nichts essen, was . . . enthält.	I can't eat anything that contains . . .
Haben Sie Gerichte für Diabetiker?	Do you have dishes for diabetics?
Haben Sie Kinderportionen?	Do you have children's portions?

Alkoholfrei
Non-alcoholic drinks

alkoholfrei
alcohol-free

der Kaffee
the coffee

koffeinfreier Kaffee
decaffeinated coffee

der Milchkaffee
the coffee with milk

der Tee
the tea

Schwarztee
black tea

Tee mit Zitrone
tea with lemon

der Kräutertee
the herbal tea

die Schokolade
the hot chocolate

das Wasser
the water

ein Wasser mit Kohlensäure
a sparkling water

die Zitronensaft
a lemonade

Alkoholfrei
Non-alcoholic drinks

ein Wasser ohne Kohlensäure
a non-sparkling water

das Mineralwasser
the mineral water

der Saft
the juice

der Granatapfelsaft
the pomegranate juice

die Apfelschorle
the apple spritzer

die Johannisbeerschorle
the red currant spritzer

Schlüsselsätze	Key phrases
Eine Flasche Mineralwasser, bitte.	A bottle of mineral water, please.
Ich möchte ein Glass Wasser mit viel Eis.	I would like a glass of water with a lot of ice.
Ohne Eis, bitte.	No ice, please.

Alkoholische Getränke
Alcoholic drinks

der Wein
the wine

der Weißwein
the white wine

der Rosé
the rosé

der Tafelwein
the table wine

die Flasche Wein
the wine bottle

das Glas
the glass

die Karaffe
the carafe

das Bier
the beer

das Bier vom Fass
the draft beer

das Malzbier
the malt beer

der Schnaps
the liquor

die Spirituosen
the spirits

Alkoholische Getränke
Alcoholic drinks

der Rum
the rum

der Apfelwein
hard cider

der Schaumwein
the sparkling wine

der Cocktail
the cocktail

der Whisky
the whiskey

der Wodka
the vodka

Schlüsselsätze	Key phrases
Ich möchte ein Bier vom Fass, bitte.	I would like a draft beer, please.
Ich möchte das hiesige Bier nehmen.	I would like the local beer.
Ich trinke keinen Alkohol.	I don't drink alcohol.
Dasselbe noch einmal, bitte.	The same again, please.
Prost!	Cheers!

Die Rechnung
The check

zahlen
to pay

die Kreditkarte
the credit card

die Quittung
the receipt

in bar zahlen
pay cash

die Rechnung
the check

Stimmt so.
No change needed.

Bitte, bitte.
You're welcome.

das Zahlterminal
the pay station

das Trinkgeld
the tip

Die Rechnung
The check

Schlüsselsätze	Key phrases
Ich möchte zahlen.	I want to pay.
Die Rechnung, bitte.	The check, please.
Und eine Quittung, bitte.	And a receipt, please.
Alles zusammen, bitte.	All together, please.
Wir möchten getrennt zahlen.	We want to pay separately.
Ist die Bedienung inbegriffen?	Is the tip included?
Stimmt so.	No change needed.

Gute Nacht!

Good night!

Das Hotel
The hotel

die Rezeption
the reception

die Zimmernummer
the room number

der Schlüssel
the key

das Gepäck
the luggage

die Abreise
the departure

das Trinkgeld
the tip

Bitte nicht stören!
Please do not disturb!

Das Hotel
The hotel

Schlüsselsätze	Key phrases
Können Sie ein Hotel in . . . empfehlen?	Can you recommend a hotel in . . . ?
Ich habe ein Zimmer reserviert.	I reserved a room.
Wir bleiben eine Woche.	We'll stay for a week.
Sie haben Zimmer Nummer 203.	Your room number is 203.
Können Sie mir bitte den Schlüssel für Zimmer . . . geben?	Could you please give me the key for room . . . ?
Gibt es Zimmerservice?	Is there room service?

Das Gästehaus und die Herberge
The bed & breakfast and the hostel

das Gasthaus
inn

der Besitzer
the owner

Frühstück inklusive
breakfast included

Schlüsselsätze	Key phrases
Was für ein Zimmer möchten Sie gern?	What kind of room would you like?
Ich hätte gern ein Zimmer mit zwei Einzelbetten.	I would like a room with two single beds.
Ich hätte gern ein Zimmer mit Bad.	I would like a room with a bathroom.
Was kostet ein Zimmer mit Vollpension?	How much is a room with full board?
Was kostet ein Zimmer mit Halbpension?	How much is a room with half board?
Wann wird das Frühstück serviert?	When is breakfast served?

Der Campingplatz
The campground

der Wohnwagen
the camper

das Wohnmobil
the RV

das Zelt
the tent

der Schlafsack
the sleeping bag

die Isomatte
the sleeping mat

die Toiletten
the toilets

die Mülleimer
the trash cans

das Lagerfeuer
the campfire

das Trinkwasser
the drinking water

die Thermosflasche
the thermos

der Kocher
the stove

die Taschenlampe
the flashlight

Die Jugendherberge
The youth hostel

voll belegt
no vacancy

der Rucksack
the backpack

warmes Wasser
hot water

Schlüsselsätze	Key phrases
Ich möchte gern ein Zimmer für . . . Nächte reservieren.	I want to reserve a room for . . . nights.
Ich möchte gern ein Zimmer vom 11. 3. bis zum 15. 3. reservieren.	I want to reserve a room from 3/11 to 3/15.
Was kostet das Zimmer pro Nacht?	How much is the room per night?
Was kostet eine Übernachtung mit Frühstück?	How much is one night with breakfast?
Bis wann müssen wir das Zimmer räumen?	When do we have to check out?
Können wir unser Gepäck bis . . . Uhr hier lassen?	Can we leave our luggage here until . . . o'clock?
Können wir bitte unser Gepäck haben?	May we get our luggage?

Der Campingplatz
The campground

das Fernglas
the binoculars

das Taschenmesser
the pocket knife

Schlüsselsätze	Key phrases
Dürfen wir hier zelten?	May we camp here?
Ich möchte einen campsite für drei Tage.	I would like a tent space for three days.
Wie viel kostet das pro Tag ?	How much does this cost per day?

Privatunterkunft
Private accommodations

die Wohnung
the apartment

das Haus
the house

das Zimmer
the room

voll möbliert
fully furnished

der Hausbesitzer
the homeowner

die Miete
the rent

die Kaution
the security deposit

die Schlüsselübergabe
the key delivery

die Klimaanlage
the air-conditioning system

das Licht
the light

die Heizung
the heater

der Balkon
the balcony

Privatunterkunft
Private accommodations

das Stockwerk
the floor

der Aufzug
the elevator

der Garten
the garden

die Treppe
the stairs

die Spülmaschine
the dishwasher

die Waschmaschine
the washing machine

der Wäschetrockner
the dryer

der Staubsauger
the vacuum cleaner

die Mülltrennung
waste separation and recycling

Privatunterkunft
Private accommodations

Schlüsselsätze	Key phrases
Von wann bis wann möchten Sie ein Zimmer reservieren?	From when to when would you like to reserve a room?
Wir werden morgen kommen.	We will arrive tomorrow.
Könnte ich noch eine Nacht bleiben?	Could I stay another night?

Die Betten
The beds

ein Einzelzimmer
a single room

ein Doppelzimmer
a double room

zwei Einzelbetten
two single beds

ein Doppelbett
a double bed

das Bett
the bed

die Matratze
the mattress

die Decke
the blanket

das Kopfkissen
the pillow

Ausstattung und Service
Furnishings and service

der Zimmerservice
the room service

das Bad
the bathroom

das Kabelfernsehen
the cable TV

das Satellitenfernsehen
the satellite TV

das Telefon
the telephone

das Internet
the Internet

das Wi-Fi
the Wi-Fi

der Aufzug
the elevator

Zugang für Behinderte
access for people with disabilities

eine Klimaanlage
an air-conditioning system

eine Minibar
a minibar

eine Sauna
a sauna

Ausstattung und Service
Furnishings and service

ein Schwimmbad
a swimming pool

ein Wäschedienst
a laundry service

die Garage
the garage

der Parkplatz
the parking lot

Das Badezimmer
The bathroom

die Dusche
the shower

die Badewanne
the bathtub

das Waschbecken
the sink

die Seife
the soap

das Duschgel
the shower gel

das Shampoo
the shampoo

die Handtücher
the towels

der Waschlappen
the washcloth

die Zahnbürste
the toothbrush

die Zahnpasta
the toothpaste

der Föhn
the blowdryer

der Kamm
the comb

Das Badezimmer
The bathroom

das Gel
the gel

die Bürste
the brush

das Parfüm
the perfume

die Köpermilch
the body lotion

der Badevorleger
the bath mat

die Heizung
the heater

der Rasierschaum
the shaving cream

der Rasierapparat
the razor

der elektrische Rasierapparat
the electric razor

die Toilette
the toilet

das Toilettenpapier
the toilet paper

der Spiegel
the mirror

Viel Spaß!

Let's Go Out!

Wie viel kostet das?
How much does it cost?

der Preis
the price

kaufen
to buy

kostenlos
free

gebührenpflichtig
charges apply

billig/günstig
cheap/inexpensive

teuer
expensive

Eintritt frei
free admission

der Schlussverkauf
the clearance sale

Wie viel kostet das?
How much does it cost?

Schlüsselsätze	**Key phrases**
Was kostet . . . ?	What does it . . . cost?
Wie viel kostet . . . ?	How much does . . . cost?
Die Geheimzahl eingeben.	Enter your PIN.
Bitte geben Sie Ihre Geheimzahl ein.	Please enter your PIN.

Money

Münzen, Geldscheine und die Bankkarte

Coins, bills and the bank card

das Bargeld
the cash

die Münze
the coin

der Schein
the bill

die Kreditkarte
the credit card

das Zahlterminal
the pay station

zahlen
to pay

der Kassenzettel
the receipt

der Geldautomat
the ATM

die Karte einführen
insert the card

abheben
get cash

die Bank
the bank

Münzen, Geldscheine und die Bankkarte
Coins, bills and the bank card

Schlüsselsätze	Key phrases
Ich möchte Euros in Schweizer Franken einwechseln/tauschen.	I want to exchange euros for Swiss francs.
Wie ist der Wechselkurs?	What is the exchange rate?
Wie hoch sind die Gebühren?	What are the fees?
Geldautomat außer Betrieb.	ATM out of service.
Wie hätten Sie das Geld gern?	How would you like the money?
In Zehnern/in Zwanzigern/ in Fünfzigern/in Hundertern, bitte.	In tens/in twenties/in fifties/in hundreds, please.
Die Karte ist ungültig/ Die Karte ist nicht zugelassen.	This card is invalid. This card is not accepted.
Die Karte wurde einbehalten. Bitte kommen Sie an den Schalter.	The card was withheld. Please come to the counter.

Kleine Geschäfte
Small stores

geöffnet
open

geschlossen
closed

das Lebensmittelgeschäft
the grocery store

der Markt
the market

der Gemüseladen
the greengrocer

die Bäckerei
the bakery

die Konditorei
the pastry shop

die Metzgerei
the butcher's shop

das Fischgeschäft
the fish shop

die Weinhandlung
the wine store

das Schuhgeschäft
the shoe store

the clothing store
die Boutique

Kleine Geschäfte
Small stores

die Buchhandlung
the bookstore

der Waschsalon
the laundromat

das Kaufhaus
the department store

der Aufzug
the elevator

die Rolltreppe
the escalator

im Erdgeschoss
on the ground floor

im Untergeschoss
in the basement

die Umkleidekabinen
the changing rooms

Kleine Geschäfte
Small stores

Schlüsselsätze	Key phrases
Wann öffnen Sie?	When do you open?
Wann schließen Sie?	When do you close?
Haben Sie mittags geöffnet?	Are you open during lunch?
Um wie viel Uhr schließen Sie am Samstag?	What time do you close on Saturdays?
Wo bekomme ich . . . ?	Where can I get . . . ?
Wo finde ich Schuhe, bitte?	Where can I find shoes, please?
Wo ist der Aufzug, bitte?	Where is the elevator, please?
Entschuldigen Sie, bitte, wo finde ich Wintermäntel?	Excuse me, please, where can I find winter coats?
Wo sind die Umkleidekabinen?	Where are the changing rooms?
. . . führen wir nicht.	We don't carry . . .

Der Supermarkt
The supermarket

der Einkaufswagen
the shopping cart

der Einkaufskorb
the shopping basket

die Abteilung
the department

die Backwaren
the baked goods

der Käse
the cheese

das Gemüse
the vegetables

der Fisch
the fish

das Fleisch
the meat

das Obst
the fruit

die Getränke
the drinks

die Spirituosen
the spirits

der Preis
the price

Der Supermarkt
The supermarket

die Kasse
the cash register

die Kassiererin
the cashier

der Kassenbon
the receipt

die Tüte
the bag

Der Supermarkt
The supermarket

Schlüsselsätze	Key phrases
Ich hätte gern ein Kilo Äpfel.	I would like a kilo of apples.
Ich hätte gern ein/zwei Pfund.	I would like one/two pound(s).
Ich hätte gern einhundert Gramm.	I would like one hundred grams.
Ich hätte gern ein/zwei Stück.	I would like one/two piece(s).
Ich hätte gern eine Scheibe/zwei Scheiben.	I would like one slice/two slices.
Hier ist meine Karte.	Here is my card.

Die Geschenke
The gifts

das Geschenk
the gift

das Reiseandenken
the souvenir

das Geschenkpapier
the wrapping paper

Gewerbe und Handwerk
Commerce and crafts

der Bierkrug
the beer mug

die Flasche Wein
the wine bottle

die Miniatur
the miniature

das Fachwerkhaus
the timber-frame house

das Schneidebrett für das Abendbrot
the cutting board for dinner

die Räuchermännchen
the incense-smoking figures

das Marzipan
the marzipan

die Töpferware
the pottery

die Bildhauerei
the sculpture

Münzen und Medaillen
coins and medals

antikes Glas und Porzellan
antique glass and porcelain

Antiquitäten und Trödel
antiques and junk

Gewerbe und Handwerk
Commerce and crafts

die Puppen
the dolls

die Zeichnung
the drawing

das Bild
the picture

die Postkarten
the postcards

der Kristall
the crystal

124

Gewerbe und Handwerk
Commerce and crafts

Schlüsselsätze	Key phrases
Suchen Sie etwas Bestimmtes?	Are you looking for something in particular?
Kann ich Ihnen behilflich sein?	Can I help you?
Ich möchte mich nur umsehen.	I'm just looking.
Ich sammle . . .	I collect . . .
Ich interessiere mich für . . .	I'm interested in . . .

Die Kleidung
Clothing

der Slip
underwear

die Unterhose
the panties

der BH
the bra

die Strumpfhose
the pantyhose

das Kostüm
the suit

die Socken
the socks

die Bluse
the blouse

das Kleid
the dress

der Rock
the skirt

der Pullover
the sweater

die Jacke
the jacket

die Regenjacke
the rain jacket

Die Kleidung
Clothing

der Blazer
the blazer

der Mantel
the coat

die Daunenjacke
the down jacket

die Hose
the pants

die Jeans
the jeans

das Unterhemd
the undershirt

die kurze Hose
the shorts

das Hemd
the shirt

das T-Shirt
the T-shirt

der Anzug
the suit

die Seide
the silk

Die Kleidung
Clothing

die Wolle
the wool

die Baumwolle
the cotton

das Leinen
the linen

das Leder
the leather

der Samt
the velvet

gestreift
striped

kariert
checkered

geblümt
floral

gepunktet
with dots

einfarbig
monochrome

sportlich
sporty

elegant
elegant

Die Kleidung
Clothing

schwarz
black

weiß
white

rot
red

grün
green

grau
grey

braun
brown

gelb
yellow

blau
blue

orange
orange

rosa
pink

violett
violet

129

Die Kleidung
Clothing

Schlüsselsätze	Key phrases
Würden Sie mir bitte helfen? Ich suche . . .	Could you help me, please? I'm looking for . . .
Aber gern, hier entlang bitte.	Of course, come this way.
Welche Größe suchen Sie?	What size do you need?
Welche Farbe soll es sein?	What color would you like?
Wie gefällt Ihnen diese Farbe?	How do you like this color?
Passt . . . ?	Does . . . fit?
Wie passt . . . ?	How does . . . fit?
Gefällt Ihnen . . . ?	Do you like . . . ?
Nein, . . . ist zu lang/kurz/ eng/weit/groß/klein.	No, . . . is too long/short/ tight/wide/big/small.
Können Sie mir eine andere Größe bringen?	Could you bring me another size?
. . . passt sehr gut.	. . . fits very well.
. . . steht mir.	. . . looks good on me.
. . . gefällt mir.	I like . . .
Ich nehme . . .	I'll take . . .

Die Schuhe
The shoes

die Stiefel
the boots

die Gummistiefel
the rubber boots

die Tennisschuhe
the tennis shoes

die Turnschuhe
the sneakers

die Pumps
the pumps

die Ballerinas
the ballet flats

die Sandalen
the sandals

die Pantoffeln
the slippers

die Hausschuhe
the house shoes

die hohen Absätze
the high heels

die flachen Absätze
the flat heels

die Wanderschuhe
the hiking shoes

Die Schuhe
The shoes

die Schuhcreme
the shoe polish

die Schnürsenkel
the shoelaces

Schlüsselsätze	Key phrases
Kann ich . . . anprobieren?	Can I try . . .
Möchten Sie . . . anprobieren?	Would you like to try . . . ?
Die grünen Schuhe sind teurer als die weißen.	The green shoes are more expensive than the white ones.

Die Accessoires
The accessories

die Handschuhe
the gloves

die Mütze
the cap

der Schal
the shawl

der Hut
the hat

der Gürtel
the belt

das Halstuch
the scarf

die Krawatte
the tie

der Rucksack
the backpack

die Handtasche
the handbag

die Brieftasche
the wallet

der Geldbeutel
a woman's wallet

die Sonnenbrille
the sunglasses

Die Accessoires
The accessories

die Schirmmütze
the baseball cap

die Strümpfe
the stockings

der Regenschirm
the umbrella

die Ohrringe
the earrings

die Halskette
the necklace

das Armband
the bracelet

die Uhr
the watch

der Ring
the ring

der Ehering
the wedding ring

die Kette
the chain

Im Freien
Outdoors

der Berg
the mountain

Ski/Schi fahren
skiing

das Rodeln
sledding

die Schneeschuhe
the snowshoes

das Bergsteigen
mountain climbing

die Hütte
the hut

der Pulverschnee
the powdery snow

die Schlucht
the ravine

das Seil
the rope

die Seilbahn
the cable car

der Sessellift
the chairlift

die Tour
the tour

Im Freien
Outdoors

wandern
hiking

radfahren
biking

das Gleitschirmfliegen
paragliding

das Fallschirmspringen
skydiving

das Kanu
the canoe

rudern
rowing

die Regatta
the regatta

angeln
fishing

das Jogging
jogging

das Segeln
sailing

das Surfen
surfing

der Fußball
soccer ball

Im Freien
Outdoors

der Fußballplatz
the soccer pitch

die Mannschaft
the team

das Spiel
the game

gewinnen
winning

die Halbzeit
halftime

der Schiedsrichter
the referee

das Rugby
rugby

das Golf
golf

die Leichtathletik
track and field

reiten
horseback riding

das Tennis
tennis

der Tennisball
the tennis ball

137

Im Freien
Outdoors

der Tennisplatz
the tennis court

der Tennisschläger
the tennis racket

Schlüsselsätze	Key phrases
Spielst du Tennis?	Do you play tennis?
Ich spiele gern Tennis.	I like playing tennis.
Ich jogge gern.	I like to go jogging.
Ich laufe gern Ski.	I like skiing.
Gibt es Wanderwege?	Are there hiking trails?
Wir wollen wandern gehen.	We want to go hiking.
Ich will bergsteigen.	I want to go mountain climbing.

Drinnen
Indoors

das Yoga
yoga

das Judo
judo

der Volleyball
volleyball -

der Basketball
basketball

der Handball
handball

das Badminton
badminton

das Turnen
gymnastics

das Squash
squash

das Tischtennis
table tennis

Am Strand
At the beach

der Strand
the beach

das Meer
the ocean

die Küste
the coast

der Wind
the wind

die Welle
the wave

die Ebbe
the low tide

die Flut
the high tide

der Badeanzug
the bathing suit

die Badehose
the swimming trunks

der Bikini
the bikini

die Schirmmütze
the baseball cap

die Sonnencreme
the suntan lotion

Am Strand
At the beach

die Sonnenbrille
the sunglasses

der Strohhut
the straw hat

das Strandtuch
the beach towel

die Strandtasche
the beach bag

der Sonnenschirm
the umbrella

der Schwimmreifen
the inner tube

der Bademeister
the lifeguard

schwimmen
swimming

die Luftmatratze
the air mattress

die Taucherbrille
the diving mask

die Schwimmflossen
the flippers

die Dusche
the shower

Am Strand
At the beach

das Tauchen
diving

der Drachen
the kite

die Sandburg
the sand castle

der Eimer
the bucket

die Schaufel
the shovel

die Düne
the dune

segeln
sailing

sich sonnen
sunbathing

das Tretboot
the pedal boat

Windsurfen gehen
windsurfing

Am Strand
At the beach

Schlüsselsätze	Key phrases
Ich segle gern.	I like to sail.
Ich gehe gern Windsurfen.	I like to windsurf.
Ich habe noch nie getaucht.	I have never dived before.
Kann man Unterricht nehmen?	Can I get lessons?
Baden verboten!	Swimming prohibited!

Im Schwimmbad
At the pool

das Schwimmbad
the pool

die Schwimmbrille
the swimming goggles

die Badekappe
the swimming cap

das Handtuch
the towel

das Schwimmbrett
the kick board

die Schwimmflossen
the flippers

der Bademeister
the lifeguard

die Dusche
the shower

Im Schwimmbad
At the pool

Schlüsselsätze	Key phrases
Ich schwimme gern.	I like to swim.
Können Sie schwimmen?	Can you swim?
Gibt es ein Freibad?	Is there an outdoor pool?

Das Kino
The cinema

die Kinokasse
the box office

der Platz
the seat

der Spielfilm
the feature film

die Vorstellung
the performance

die Eintrittskarte
the ticket

das Drehbuch
the script

die Szene
the scene

Das Kino
The cinema

Schlüsselsätze	Key phrases
Ich möchte einen Film sehen.	I want to watch a film.
In welchem Kino läuft . . . ?	In which theater is . . . playing?
Um wie viel Uhr beginnt die Vorstellung?	At what time does it start?
Läuft der Film im Original oder ist er synchronisiert?	Is the film in the original language or dubbed?
Wie war der Film?	How was the film?
Hat euch der Film gefallen?	Did you like the film?

Das Theater
The theater

die Theaterkarte
the theater ticket

der Schauspieler
the actor

die Schauspielerin
the actress

der Beifall
the applause

die Theaterkasse
the box office

der Platz
the seat

Die Oper
The theater

das Opernhaus
the opera house

die Galavorstellung
the gala performance

der Dirigent
the conductor

die Parkettplätze
the orchestra seats

die Operette
the operetta

das Ballett
the ballet

der Tänzer
the dancer (male)

die Tänzerin
the dancer (female)

die Pause
the intermission

der Sänger
the singer (male)

die Sängerin
the singer (female)

Die Oper
The theater

Schlüsselsätze	Key phrases
Ich möchte . . . Karten für . . .	I would like . . . tickets for . . .
Habt ihr Karten für die Matinee gekauft?	Did you buy tickets for the matinee?
Gibt es noch Plätze im Parkett?	Are any orchestra seats left?
Ich hätte Lust ins Ballett zu gehen.	I would like to go to the ballet.

Das Museum
The museum

die Öffnungszeiten
the opening hours

die Ausstellung
the exhibition

die Bildhauerei
the sculpture

die Malerei
the painting

die Kunst
the art

die Architektur
the architecture

das Töpfern
the pottery

die Fotografie
the photography

Das Museum
The museum

Schlüsselsätze	Key phrases
Ich möchte die . . . Ausstellung sehen.	I want to see the . . . exhibition.
In welchem Museum gibt es die . . . Ausstellung?	In which museum is the . . . exhibition?
Ist das Museum sonntags geöffnet?	Is the museum open on Sundays?
Um wie viel Uhr öffnet das Museum?	At what time does the museum open?
Möchten Sie eine Sonderausstellung sehen?	Would you like to see a special exhibition?
Die Ausstellung hat mir sehr gut gefallen.	I liked the exhibition very much.
Ich interessiere mich für Bildhauerei.	I'm interested in sculpture.
Wir waren heute Morgen im Kunstmuseum.	We were at the art museum this morning.

Die Musik
The music

das Konzert
the concert

der Konzertsal
the concert hall

die Party
the party

das Publikum
the audience

die Bar
the bar

die Disko
the nightclub

der Tanz
the dance

die Kneipe
the pub

die Show
the show

das Orchester
the orchestra

der Chor
the choir

die Musik
the music

Die Musik
The music

die Flöte
recorders

die Gitarre
the guitar

die Trompete
the trumpet

das Klavier
the piano

die Geige
the violin

das Akkordeon
the accordion

Die Musik
The music

Schlüsselsätze	Key phrases
Ich möchte ins Konzert gehen.	I want to go to the concert.
Wann findet die Party statt?	What time is the party?
Wo findet die Party statt?	Where is the party?
Nein, da kann ich leider nicht. Ich habe schon etwas anderes vor.	Sorry, I can't go at that time. I already have other plans.
Wir haben uns ausgezeichnet unterhalten.	We had an excellent conversation.
Die Party war fantastisch.	The party was fantastic.

Achtung!

Watch out!

Der menschliche Körper
The human body

der Kopf
the head

die Brust
the chest

die Brüste
the breasts

der Hals
the neck

der Arm
the arm

die Hand
the hand

das Handgelenk
the wrist

der Finger
the finger

der Daumen
the thumb

der Rücken
the back

die Schulter
the shoulder

der Ellbogen
the elbow

Der menschliche Körper
The human body

der Bauch
the belly

das Bein
the leg

das Knie
the knee

das Fußgelenk
the ankle

der Fuß
the foot

der Zeh
the toe

die Wirbelsäule
the spine

der Muskel
the muscle

das Herz
the heart

der Knochen
the bone

der Magen
the stomach

die Lunge
the lungs

Der menschliche Körper
The human body

das Gehirn
the brain

die Leber
the liver

die Nieren
the kidneys

Der menschliche Körper
The human body

Schlüsselsätze	Key phrases
Ich habe Rückenschmerzen.	I have back pain.
Mir tut der Bauch weh.	I have a stomachache.
Ich habe Schmerzen im Arm.	My arm hurts.

Das Gesicht
The face

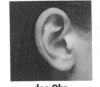

das Gesicht
the face

die Stirn
the forehead

die Lippen
the lips

das Ohr
the ear

die Haare

die Haare
the hair

die Augen
the eyes

der Mund
the mouth

die Zunge
the tongue

rote/schwarze/blonde Haare
red/black/blonde hair

die Nase
the nose

der Kiefer
the jaw

die Zähne
the teeth

Das Gesicht
The face

das Kinn
the chin

ein Bart/bartlos
a beard/no beard

das Lid
the eyelid

die Pupille
the pupil

eine Glatze
a bald head

die Brille
the glasses

Schlüsselsätze	Key phrases
Machen Sie bitte den Mund auf.	Please open your mouth.
Ich habe Halsschmerzen.	I have a sore throat.
Ich habe Kopfschmerzen/ Zahnschmerzen.	I have a headache/ toothache.

Ärzte
The doctors

die Arztpraxis
the doctor's office

der Arzt.(m)/die Ärztin(f)
the doctor

der Augenarzt
the ophthalmologist

der Hautarzt
the dermatologist

der HNO-Arzt
the ENT physician

der Kinderarzt
the pediatrician

die Zahnärztin
the dentist

die Krankheit
the disease

die Krankenkasse
the health insurance

der Krankenschein
certificate of illness

Ärzte
The doctors

Schlüsselsätze	Key phrases
Holen Sie einen Arzt!	Get a doctor!
Ich brauche einen Arzt.	I need a doctor.
Wo ist die nächste Arztpraxis?	Where is the nearest doctor's office?
Ich bin allergisch gegen . . .	I'm allergic to . . .
Ich bin schwanger.	I'm pregnant.
Ich bin Diabetiker.	I'm diabetic.
Ich bin Epileptiker.	I'm epileptic.
Ich habe ein Herzleiden.	I have a heart condition.
Ich habe zu hohen/ niedrigen Blutdruck.	My blood pressure is too high/low.
Atmen Sie bitte tief durch.	Please take a deep breath.
Husten Sie bitte.	Please cough.

Patienten und Krankheitssymptome
Patients and symptoms

schwanger
pregnant

der Diabetiker
the diabetic

der Epileptiker
the epileptic

der Asthmatiker
the asthmatic

die Allergie
the allergy

die Übelkeit
the nausea

das Fieber
the fever

der Husten
the cough

der Schnupfen
the runny nose

der Schmerz
the pain

die Kopfschmerzen
the headache

die Halsschmerzen
the sore throat

Patienten und Krankheitssymptome
Patients and symptoms

die Zahnschmerzen
the toothache

die Rückenschmerzen
the back pain

das Sodbrennen
the heartburn

die Verletzung
the Injury

der Bruch
the fracture

der Heuschnupfen
the hay fever

der Schnitt
the cut

die Blutung
the bleeding

der Sonnenbrand
the sunburn

der Ausschlag
the rash

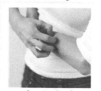
der Juckreiz
the itching

Patienten und Krankheitssymptome
Patients and symptoms

Schlüsselsätze	Key phrases
Ich fühle mich nicht wohl.	I don't feel well.
Ich bin krank.	I'm sick.
Ich habe Fieber.	I have a fever.
Mir ist übel.	I'm nauseous.
Ich habe mich übergeben.	I vomited.
Ich habe Durchfall.	I have diarrhea.
Ich habe Asthma.	I have asthma.

Die Apotheke und die Medikamente
The pharmacy and the medicine

die Apotheke
the pharmacy

das Medikament
the medicine

das Schmerzmittel
the pain reliever

die Tabletten
the tablets

das Antibiotikum
the antibiotic

Das Plaster
the adhesive bandage

das Desinfektionsmittel
the disinfectant

das Thermometer
the thermometer

der Hustensaft
the cough syrup

das Rezept
the prescription

das Kondom
the condom

das Aspirin
aspirin

Die Apotheke und die Medikamente
The pharmacy and the medicine

die Nasentropfen
the nose drops

der Verband
the bandage (plaster)

die Spritze
the syringe

die Salbe
the ointment

die Schlaftablette
the sleeping pill

das Abführmittel
the laxative

Die Apotheke und die Medikamente
The pharmacy and the medicine

Schlüsselsätze	Key phrases
Nehmen Sie noch andere Medikamente?	Do you take any other medicine?
Bitte, nehmen Sie . . . Tabletten/Teelöffel . . .	Please take . . . tablets/teaspoons . . .
Dreimal am Tag/täglich.	Three times a day/daily.
Vor/nach dem Essen.	Before/after a meal.
Ich habe ein Rezept für dieses Medikament.	I have a prescription for this medicine.
Ich habe keine Medikamente mehr.	I don't have any more medicine.

Das Krankenhaus
The hospital

die Notaufnahme
the emergency room

die Röntgenaufnahme
the X-ray

das Wartezimmer
the waiting room

die Temperatur
the temperature

der Blutdruck
the blood pressure

**die ärztliche
Untersuchung**
the medical exam

Das Krankenhaus
The hospital

Schlüsselsätze	Key phrases
Wo ist das nächste Krankenhaus?	Where is the nearest hospital?
Ich bin verletzt.	I'm injured.
Spricht hier jemand Deutsch?	Does anyone speak German here?
Was haben Sie für Beschwerden?	What are your symptoms?
Wo tut es weh?	Where does it hurt?
Tut es hier weh?	Does it hurt here?
Wie lange fühlen Sie sich schon so?	How long have you felt like this?
Sind Sie gegen irgendetwas allergisch?	Are you allergic to anything?

Die Polizei
The police

der Diebstahl
the theft

**meine Brieftasche/
mein**
my wallet

meine Tasche
my bag

mein Geld
my money

mein Pass
my passport

mein Auto
my car

Ich bin verletzt.
I'm injured.

Es gibt Verletzte.
There are injured people.

Die Polizei
The police

Schlüsselsätze

Key phrases

Hilfe!
Help!

Haltet den Dieb!
Stop the thief!

Rufen Sie die Polizei!
Call the police!

Wo ist die nächste Polizeiwache?
Where is the nearest police station?

Ich möchte einen Diebstahl/ Raubüberfall melden.
I want to report a theft/hold-up.

Man hat bei mir eingebrochen.
Someone broke into my place.

Man hat mein Auto aufgebrochen.
My car was broken into.

Ich möchte einen Unfall melden.
I want to report an accident.

Holen Sie einen Arzt!
Call a doctor!

Ich möchte einen Unfall auf der Autobahn melden.
I want to report an accident on the motorway.

Rufen Sie einen Krankenwagen!
Call an ambulance!

Rufen Sie die Feuerwehr!
Call the fire department!

Feuer!
Fire!

Es gibt Verletzte.
There are injured people.

Ich brauche einen Anwalt.
I need a lawyer.

Ich möchte das Konsulat anrufen.
I want to call the consulate.

Chapter 01

Page 12: alice_photo/Adobe Stock Photos, muratart/Adobe Stock Photos, Racle Fotodesign/Adobe Stock Photos, Monkey Business/Adobe Stock Photos, BillionPhotos.com/Adobe Stock Photos, adisa/Adobe Stock Photos, Room 76 Photography/Adobe Stock Photos, monticellllo/Adobe Stock Photos, sumroeng/Adobe Stock Photos, airborne77/Adobe Stock Photos, pressmaster/Adobe Stock Photos, robin2b/Adobe Stock Photos.

Page 13: Inkara/Adobe Stock Photos, Rido/Adobe Stock Photos, RioPatuca Images/Adobe Stock Photos, terovesalainen/Adobe Stock Photos, Artem/Adobe Stock Photos, Robert Wilson/Adobe Stock Photos, Francesco Scatena/Adobe Stock Photos, Rawpixel.com/Adobe Stock Photos, Lotfi MATTOU/Adobe Stock Photos, gstockstudio/Adobe Stock Photos, dell/Adobe Stock Photos, nadezhda1906/Adobe Stock Photos.

Page 14: vitaliymateha/Adobe Stock Photos, euthymia/Adobe Stock Photos, Falcon Eyes/Adobe Stock Photos, italita/Adobe Stock Photos, phaisarnwong2517/Adobe Stock Photos, blacksalmon/Adobe Stock Photos, xy/Adobe Stock Photos, vahekatrjyan/Adobe Stock Photos.

Page 16: kameraauge/Adobe Stock Photos, mayabuns/Adobe Stock Photos, jarma/Adobe Stock Photos, Scanrail/Adobe Stock Photos, NWM/Adobe Stock Photos, sultan/Adobe Stock Photos, Alice Slee/Adobe Stock Photos, Alessandro Cristiano/Adobe Stock Photos, Nikolai Sorokin/Adobe Stock Photos, jotily/Adobe Stock Photos, Ysr/Adobe Stock Photos, artmim/Adobe Stock Photos.

Page 17: pakorn/Adobe Stock Photos, adrian_ilie825/Adobe Stock Photos, kasto/Adobe Stock Photos, Sven Grundmann/Adobe Stock Photos, MaxPhotoArt/Adobe Stock Photos, Daniel Ernst/Adobe Stock Photos, pressmaster/Adobe Stock Photos, terovesalainen/Adobe Stock Photos, jdoms/Adobe Stock Photos, #CNF/Adobe Stock Photos, Kzenon/Adobe Stock Photos, Yakobchuk Olena/Adobe Stock Photos.

Page 18: littleny/Adobe Stock Photos, Vincent Bouchet/Adobe Stock Photos, nerthuz/Adobe Stock Photos, M. Schuppich/Adobe Stock Photos, gonin/Adobe Stock Photos, Felix Jork/Adobe Stock Photos, Photo by form PxHere, nerthuz/Adobe Stock Photos.

Page 20: Konstantinos Moraiti/Adobe Stock Photos, flatvectors/ Adobe Stock Photos, Destina/Adobe Stock Photos, New Africa/Adobe Stock Photos, mipan/Adobe Stock Photos, Sashkin/Adobe Stock Photos, accurate_shot/Adobe Stock Photos, Ayzek/Adobe Stock Photos, kupchynskyi12/Adobe Stock Photos, black_magic/Adobe Stock Photos, GTeam/Adobe Stock Photos, fotofabrika/Adobe Stock Photos.

Page 21: Jürgen Fälchle/Adobe Stock Photos, Laz'e-Pete/Adobe Stock Photos, Pixabay, Nickolay Khoroshkov/Adobe Stock Photos, sp4764/ Adobe Stock Photos, Sergey Yarochkin/Adobe Stock Photos, rachid amrous/Adobe Stock Photos, biggi62/Adobe Stock Photos, rachid amrous/Adobe Stock Photos, peteri/Adobe Stock Photos, Anton Gvozdikov/Adobe Stock Photos, Markus Mainka/Adobe Stock Photos.

Page 22: helenedevun/Adobe Stock Photos, Marem/Adobe Stock Photos, Comofoto/Adobe Stock Photos, Unclesam/Adobe Stock Photos, VanderWolf Images/Adobe Stock Photos, Frederic Bos/Adobe Stock Photos, Pascal Martin/Adobe Stock Photos, Adrien Roussel/Adobe Stock Photos, travelview/Adobe Stock Photos, fabiomax/Adobe Stock Photos, digitalstock/Adobe Stock Photos.

Page 24: JackF/Adobe Stock Photos, Oleg/Adobe Stock Photos, algre/Adobe Stock Photos, Andrey_Lobachev/Adobe Stock Photos, Konstantinos Moraiti/Adobe Stock Photos, MTG/Adobe Stock Photos, Maksim Toome/Adobe Stock Photos, algre/Adobe Stock Photos, ivanko80/Adobe Stock Photos, Flamingo Images/Adobe Stock Photos, Andrey Popov/Adobe Stock Photos, Daylight Photo/Adobe Stock Photos.

Page 26: tournee/Adobe Stock Photos, jojoo64/Adobe Stock Photos, Kzenon/Adobe Stock Photos.

Page 27: stockphoto-graf/Adobe Stock Photos, Jiri Hera/Adobe Stock Photos, nito/Adobe Stock Photos, stockphoto-graf/Adobe Stock Photos, rotoGraphics/Adobe Stock Photos, moonrise/Adobe Stock Photos, lastfurianec/Adobe Stock Photos, stockphoto-graf/Adobe Stock Photos, jufo/Adobe Stock Photos, Winai Tepsuttinun/Adobe Stock Photos, philip kinsey/Adobe Stock Photos, Richard Villalon/Adobe Stock Photos.

Page 28: PUNTOSTUDIOFOTO Lda/Adobe Stock Photos, Photobeps/ Adobe Stock Photos, ekostsov/Adobe Stock Photos, nkarol/Adobe Stock Photos, MIGUEL GARCIA SAAVED/Adobe Stock Photos.

Chapter 02

Page 30: Cookie Studio/Adobe Stock Photos, Sergey Novikov/Adobe Stock Photos, be free/Adobe Stock Photos, Antonioguillem/Adobe Stock Photos, Cookie Studio/Adobe Stock Photos, jackfrog/Adobe Stock Photos, sveta/Adobe Stock Photos, Maridav/Adobe Stock Photos.

Page 32: iuricazac/Adobe Stock Photos, Viacheslav Iakobchuk/Adobe Stock Photos, Wayhome Studio/Adobe Stock Photos, michaelheim/Adobe Stock Photos, fotogestoeber/Adobe Stock Photos, smallblackcat/Adobe Stock Photos, Wayhome Studio/Adobe Stock Photos, vladimirfloyd/Adobe Stock Photos.

Page 33: Cookie Studio/Adobe Stock Photos, Maridav/Adobe Stock Photos, detailblick-foto/Adobe Stock Photos, Roman Babakin/Adobe Stock Photos, auremar/Adobe Stock Photos, shurkin_son/Adobe Stock Photos, william87/Adobe Stock Photos.

Page 35: hin255/Adobe Stock Photos, Oleksandr Moroz/Adobe Stock Photos, Drobot Dean/Adobe Stock Photos, Chepko Danil/Adobe Stock Photos, Photo by Djim Loic on Unsplash, devenorr/Adobe Stock Photos, WONG SZE FEI/Adobe Stock Photos, WONG SZE FEI/Adobe Stock Photos, Prostock-studio/Adobe Stock Photos, WONG SZE FEI/Adobe Stock Photos, Priscilla Du Preez on Unsplash, Jens Ottoson/Adobe Stock Photos.

Page 36: Antonioguillem/Adobe Stock Photos, photobee/Adobe Stock Photos, oneinchpunch/Adobe Stock Photos.

Chapter 03

Page 38: auremar/Adobe Stock Photos, ivanko80/Adobe Stock Photos, Production Perig/Adobe Stock Photos, ilolab/Adobe Stock Photos, ursule/Adobe Stock Photos, rh2010/Adobe Stock Photos, Peter Brewer/Adobe Stock Photos, mk1221/Adobe Stock Photos, asab80/Adobe Stock Photos, Dmytro/Adobe Stock Photos, cantor pannatto/Adobe Stock Photos, eyetronic/Adobe Stock Photos.

Page 39: Brad Pict/Adobe Stock Photos, Johannes Beilharz on Unsplash, Marco2811/Adobe Stock Photos, samott/Adobe Stock Photos, comzeal/Adobe Stock Photos, nicknick_ko/Adobe Stock Photos, PHILETDOM/Adobe Stock Photos, kameraauge/Adobe Stock Photos, Eléonore H/Adobe Stock Photos, alice_photo/Adobe Stock Photos, shiryu01/Adobe Stock Photos, Kadmy/Adobe Stock Photos.

Page 40: pogonici/Adobe Stock Photos, rlat/Adobe Stock Photos, pressmaster/Adobe Stock Photos.

Page 41: jojoo64/Adobe Stock Photos, vladimirfloyd/Adobe Stock Photos, jojoo64/Adobe Stock Photos, methaphum/Adobe Stock Photos, Antonioguillem/Adobe Stock Photos, PictureP./Adobe Stock Photos, PictureP./Adobe Stock Photos, mantinov/Adobe Stock Photos, Jennifer Coffin-Grey on Unsplash.

Page 42: Bohdan/Adobe Stock Photos, Bohdan/Adobe Stock Photos, Bohdan/Adobe Stock Photos, Bohdan/Adobe Stock Photos, PictureP./Adobe Stock Photos, PictureP./Adobe Stock Photos, CLIPAREA. com/Adobe Stock Photos, Martino Pietropoli on Unsplash, imaginando/Adobe Stock Photos.

Page 44: Yasonya/Adobe Stock Photos, s22d/Adobe Stock Photos, jack-sooksan/Adobe Stock Photos, kmiragaya/Adobe Stock Photos, Hervé Rouveure/Adobe Stock Photos, rachid amrous/Adobe Stock Photos, Syda Productions/Adobe Stock Photos, photology1971/ Adobe Stock Photos, Laura Lévy/Adobe Stock Photos, Lucian Milasan/Adobe Stock Photos, rh2010/Adobe Stock Photos, Annette Schindler/Adobe Stock Photos.

Page 45: Fontanis/Adobe Stock Photos, Heiko Kalweit/Adobe Stock Photos, panosud360/Adobe Stock Photos, valeryegorov/Adobe Stock Photos, Hans-Martin Goede/Adobe Stock Photos, e55evu/ Adobe Stock Photos, Karen Grigoryan/Adobe Stock Photos, Iago/ Adobe Stock Photos, jotily/Adobe Stock Photos, galitskaya/Adobe Stock Photos, Adam Wasilewski/Adobe Stock Photos, Monet/Adobe Stock Photos.

Page 46: Pixabay, zhu difeng/Adobe Stock Photos.

Page 47: martialred/Adobe Stock Photos, martialred/Adobe Stock Photos, Alena/Adobe Stock Photos, photobyphotoboy/Adobe Stock Photos, Bluejayy/Adobe Stock Photos, martine wagner/Adobe Stock Photos, tradol/Adobe Stock Photos, khuruzero/Adobe Stock Photos, ozaiachin/Adobe Stock Photos.

Page 48: Bohdan/Adobe Stock Photos, marketlan/Adobe Stock Photos, Oleg/Adobe Stock Photos, Maridav/Adobe Stock Photos, Andreas/Adobe Stock Photos, Cobalt/Adobe Stock Photos, winyu/ Adobe Stock Photos, by-studio/Adobe Stock Photos, Bohdan/Adobe Stock Photos, klagyivik/Adobe Stock Photos, vladischern/Adobe Stock Photos, Olesia Bilkei/Adobe Stock Photos, Guillaume Aury/ Adobe Stock Photos.

Page 49: Olivier Tabary/Adobe Stock Photos, Antonioguillem/Adobe Stock Photos, saratm/Adobe Stock Photos, cherylvb/Adobe Stock Photos, phive2015/Adobe Stock Photos.

Page 50: John Smith/Adobe Stock Photos, zlikovec/Adobe Stock Photos, doris oberfrank-list/Adobe Stock Photos, Showcaze/Adobe Stock Photos, Pixxs/Adobe Stock Photos, by-studio/Adobe Stock Photos, sunftaka77/Adobe Stock Photos, s22d/Adobe Stock Photos, gilitukha/Adobe Stock Photos, Cmon/Adobe Stock Photos, by-studio/Adobe Stock Photos, panosud360/Adobe Stock Photos.

Page 51: Vera Kuttelvaserova/Adobe Stock Photos, Benno Hoff/Adobe Stock Photos, motivthueringen8/Adobe Stock Photos, zauberblicke/Adobe Stock Photos.

Page 52: 隆一 本田/Adobe Stock Photos, Pixabay, resuimages/Adobe Stock Photos, Mike Fouque/Adobe Stock Photos, edan/Adobe Stock Photos, Donnerbold/Adobe Stock Photos, Carl-Jürgen Bautsch/Adobe Stock Photos, annacurnow/Adobe Stock Photos, Mikhail/Adobe Stock Photos, Jürgen Fälchle/Adobe Stock Photos, soundsnaps/Adobe Stock Photos, Netzer Johannes/Adobe Stock Photos.

Page 53: lamax/Adobe Stock Photos, JFL Photography/Adobe Stock Photos, MarcoMonticone/Adobe Stock Photos, Schlierner/Adobe Stock Photos.

Chapter 04

Page 56: cdrcom/Adobe Stock Photos, leezarius/Adobe Stock Photos, orinocoArt/Adobe Stock Photos, igorkol_ter/Adobe Stock Photos, eshma/Adobe Stock Photos, vvoe/Adobe Stock Photos, vvoe/Adobe Stock Photos, volff/Adobe Stock Photos, Jiri Hera/Adobe Stock Photos.

Page 57: eyetronic/Adobe Stock Photos, PhotoKD/Adobe Stock Photos, efired/Adobe Stock Photos, Alexander Raths/Adobe Stock Photos, MarcoBagnoli Elflaco/Adobe Stock Photos, fotoknips/Adobe Stock Photos, Fischer Food Design/Adobe Stock Photos, dream79/Adobe Stock Photos, happy_lark/Adobe Stock Photos.

Page 58: fabiomax/Adobe Stock Photos, illustrez-vous/Adobe Stock Photos, Joe Gough, Arkadiusz Fajer/Adobe Stock Photos, Kimberly Reinick/Adobe Stock Photos, st-fotograf/Adobe Stock Photos, lastsurprise/Adobe Stock Photos, Elena Schweitzer/Adobe Stock Photos, Pixel-Shot/Adobe Stock Photos, karandaev/Adobe

Stock Photos, pavkis/Adobe Stock Photos, Tammajak/Adobe Stock Photos.

Page 59: tashka2000/Adobe Stock Photos, M.studio/Adobe Stock Photos, 5second/Adobe Stock Photos, Nitr/Adobe Stock Photos, pilip-photo/Adobe Stock Photos, wideonet/Adobe Stock Photos, Maxim Khytra/Adobe Stock Photos, baibaz/Adobe Stock Photos, istetiana/Adobe Stock Photos, New Africa/Adobe Stock Photos, baibaz/Adobe Stock Photos, Benjamin LEFEBVRE/Adobe Stock Photos.

Page 60: galam/Adobe Stock Photos.

Page 61: M.studio/Adobe Stock Photos, gitusik/Adobe Stock Photos, Sławomir Fajer/Adobe Stock Photos, M.studio/Adobe Stock Photos, Mara Zemgaliete/Adobe Stock, Dalmatin.o/Adobe Stock Photos, MissesJones/Adobe Stock Photos, Quade/Adobe Stock Photos, Joe Gough/Adobe Stock Photos, teleginatania/Adobe Stock Photos, guy/Adobe Stock Photos, Alexander Raths/Adobe Stock Photos.

Page 62: Maurice Metzger/Adobe Stock Photos, Viktor/Adobe Stock Photos, Mara Zemgaliete/Adobe Stock Photos, pioneer111/Adobe Stock Photos, ALF photo/Adobe Stock Photos, whitestorm/Adobe Stock Photos, diamant24/Adobe Stock Photos, Patryk Kosmider/Adobe Stock Photos, xamtiw/Adobe Stock Photos, akf/Adobe Stock Photos, Lsantilli/Adobe Stock Photos, ALF photo/Adobe Stock Photos.

Page 63: gitusik/Adobe Stock Photos, lophie/Adobe Stock Photos, Mara Zemgaliete/Adobe Stock Photos, Christian Jung/Adobe Stock Photos, Bill/Adobe Stock Photos, Marco Mayer/Adobe Stock Photos, kab-vision/Adobe Stock Photos, FOOD-pictures/Adobe Stock Photos, Maceo/Adobe Stock Photos, petzshadow/Adobe Stock Photos, pamela_d_mcadams/Adobe Stock Photos, karelnoppe/Adobe Stock Photos.

Page 64: Volodymyr Shevchuk/Adobe Stock Photos, Sergio Martínez/Adobe Stock Photos, Igor Dudchak/Adobe Stock Photos, Lana Langlois/Adobe Stock Photos, L.Bouvier/Adobe Stock Photos, Oleg Zhukov/Adobe Stock Photos.

Page 65: exclusive-design/Adobe Stock Photos, larcobasso/Adobe Stock Photos, rdnzl/Adobe Stock Photos, Silvia Bogdanski/Adobe Stock Photos, Jiri Hera/Adobe Stock Photos, Harald Biebel/Adobe Stock Photos, shibachuu/Adobe Stock Photos, Dionisvera/Adobe Stock Photos, Iurii Kachkovskyi/Adobe Stock

Photos, mbongo/Adobe Stock Photos, gavran333/Adobe Stock Photos, Birgit Reitz-Hofmann/Adobe Stock Photos.

Page 66: shibachuu/Adobe Stock Photos, Anatoly Repin/Adobe Stock Photos, mariusz_g/Adobe Stock Photos, Viktor/Adobe Stock Photos, hcast/Adobe Stock Photos, Jiri Hera/Adobe Stock Photos, rdnzl/Adobe Stock Photos, lurs/Adobe Stock Photos, Natika/Adobe Stock Photos, Valentina R./Adobe Stock Photos, Lev/Adobe Stock Photos, ChaoticDesignStudio/Adobe Stock Photos.

Page 67: imagineilona/Adobe Stock Photos, JRP Studio/Adobe Stock Photos.

Page 68: andriigorulko/Adobe Stock Photos, Jimmy/Adobe Stock Photos, osoznaniejizni/Adobe Stock Photos, ALF photo/Adobe Stock Photos, vitals/Adobe Stock Photos, Dionisvera/Adobe Stock Photos, photocrew/Adobe Stock Photos, Moving Moment/Adobe Stock Photos, kitsananan Kuna/Adobe Stock Photos.

Page 69: dream79/Adobe Stock Photos, alinamd/Adobe Stock Photos, ampFotoStudio.com/Adobe Stock Photos, unpict/Adobe Stock Photos, xalanx/Adobe Stock Photos, Lsantilli/Adobe Stock Photos, M.studio/Adobe Stock Photos, rockvillephoto/Adobe Stock Photos, Adobe Systems Incorporated, helenedevun/Adobe Stock Photos, DLeonis/Adobe Stock Photos, photocrew/Adobe Stock Photos.

Page 70: southmind/Adobe Stock Photos, M.studio/Adobe Stock Photos, viperagp/Adobe Stock Photos.

Page 71: alinamd/Adobe Stock Photos, Voravuth/Adobe Stock Photos, bergamont/Adobe Stock Photos, kolosm, Tim UR/Adobe Stock Photos, Svetlana/Adobe Stock Photos, tedestudio/Getty Images, BillionPhotos.com/Adobe Stock Photos, Tim UR/Adobe Stock Photos, seralex/Adobe Stock Photos, krasyuk/Adobe Stock Photos, atoss/Adobe Stock Photos.

Page 72: bestphotostudio/Adobe Stock Photos, yvdavid/Adobe Stock Photos, Serhiy Shullye/Adobe Stock Photos, andersphoto/Adobe Stock Photos, yvdavid/Adobe Stock Photos, alexlukin/Adobe Stock Photos, Iurii Kachkovskyi/Adobe Stock Photos, kolesnikovserg/Adobe Stock Photos, Natika/Adobe Stock Photos, Anna Sedneva/Adobe Stock Photos, kovaleva_ka/Adobe Stock Photos, akamaraqu/Adobe Stock Photos.

Page 73: Mariusz Blach/Adobe Stock Photos, Serhiy Shullye/Adobe Stock Photos, illustrez-vous/Adobe Stock Photos.

Page 74: janvier/Adobe Stock Photos, Gresei/Adobe Stock Photos, byheaven/Adobe Stock Photos, freila/Adobe Stock Photos, stefano-venturi/Adobe Stock Photos, SunnyS/Adobe Stock Photos, xamtiw/Adobe Stock Photos, Brent Hofacker/Adobe Stock Photos, luissybus-ter/Adobe Stock Photos, Scisetti Alfio/Adobe Stock Photos, Роман Фернаті/Adobe Stock Photos, andriigorulko/Adobe Stock Photos.

Page 75: Nataly-Nete/Adobe Stock Photos, Dionisvera/Adobe Stock Photos, womue/Adobe Stock Photos, constantinos/Adobe Stock Photos, margo555/Adobe Stock Photos, niteenrk/Adobe Stock Photos, Hyrma/Adobe Stock Photos, duncanandison/Adobe Stock Photos, Barbara Pheby/Adobe Stock Photos, oleh11/Adobe Stock Photos, Valentina R./Adobe Stock Photos, Superheang168/Adobe Stock Photos.

Page 76: margo555/Adobe Stock Photos, Xavier/Adobe Stock Photos, Scisetti Alfio/Adobe Stock Photos, Jörg Rautenberg/Adobe Stock Photos, nd700/Adobe Stock Photos, Viktor/Adobe Stock Photos, unpict/Adobe Stock Photos, sucharat/Adobe Stock Photos, Angel Simon/Adobe Stock Photos, Dionisvera/Adobe Stock Photos, Natika/Adobe Stock Photos.

Page 78: Konstiantyn/Adobe Stock Photos, Zerbor/Adobe Stock Photos, exclusive-design/Adobe Stock Photos, joern_gebhardt/Adobe Stock Photos, DisobeyArt/Adobe Stock Photos, Ilshat/Adobe Stock Photos, arinahablch/Adobe Stock Photos, Irina Schmidt/Adobe Stock Photos, mariolizaola/Adobe Stock Photos.

Page 80: Brian Jackson/Adobe Stock Photos, EdNurg/Adobe Stock Photos, kubais/Adobe Stock Photos, twlxx/Adobe Stock Photos, murasal/Adobe Stock Photos, Syda Productions/Adobe Stock Photos, estradaanton/Adobe Stock Photos, johnmerlin/Adobe Stock Photos, luckypic/Adobe Stock Photos.

Page 82: guy/Adobe Stock Photos, petrrgoskov/Adobe Stock Photos, FomaA/Adobe Stock Photos, GMMaria/Adobe Stock Photos, Maryna Voronova/Adobe Stock Photos, ltummy/Adobe Stock Photos, Africa Studio/Adobe Stock Photos, vitals/Adobe Stock Photos, PhotoSG/Adobe Stock Photos, andersphoto/Adobe Stock Photos, lefebvre_jonathan/Adobe Stock Photos, Barbara Pheby/Adobe Stock Photos.

Page 84: Jérôme Rommé/Adobe Stock Photos, Callozzo/Adobe Stock Photos, rcfotostock/Adobe Stock Photos, Rhönbergfoto/Adobe

Stock Photos, blende40/Adobe Stock Photos, silencefoto/Adobe Stock Photos, Harald Biebel/Adobe Stock Photos, Hakan Varli/Adobe Stock Photos, ExQuisine/Adobe Stock Photos, Olga/Adobe Stock Photos, xalanx/Adobe Stock Photos, karepa/Adobe Stock Photos.

Page 85: Katrin Linke/Adobe Stock Photos, Simone/Adobe Stock Photos, Danicek/Adobe Stock Photos, Alexander Raths/Adobe Stock Photos, lcrms/Adobe Stock Photos, Barbara Pheby/Adobe Stock Photos.

Page 86: blattwerkstatt/Adobe Stock Photos, dehweh/Adobe Stock Photos, ratmaner/Adobe Stock Photos, san_ta/Adobe Stock Photos, bit24/Adobe Stock Photos, Gstudio Group/Adobe Stock Photos, MegaSitio Design/Adobe Stock Photos, Arcady/Adobe Stock Photos, Arcady/Adobe Stock Photos.

Page 88: Marco2811/Adobe Stock Photos, dimakp/Adobe Stock Photos, NoahGolan/Adobe Stock Photos, sunwaylight13/Adobe Stock Photos, rudisetiawan/Adobe Stock Photos, rdnzl/Adobe Stock Photos, tashka2000/Adobe Stock Photos, sonyakamoz/Adobe Stock Photos, lilechka75/Adobe Stock Photos, Tim UR/Adobe Stock Photos, soleg/Adobe Stock Photos, karandaev/Adobe Stock Photos.

Page 89: alter_photo/Adobe Stock Photos, picsfive/Adobe Stock Photos, Africa Studio/Adobe Stock Photos, valery121283/Adobe Stock Photos, oxie99/Adobe Stock Photos, A_Bruno/Adobe Stock Photos.

Page 90: DenisMArt/Adobe Stock Photos, Mariyana M/Adobe Stock Photos, baibaz/Adobe Stock Photos, karapiru/Adobe Stock Photos, He2/Adobe Stock Photos, Elenathewise/Adobe Stock Photos, oscar0/Adobe Stock Photos, by-studio/Adobe Stock Photos, Weston/Adobe Stock Photos, yurakp/Adobe Stock Photos, unpict/Adobe Stock Photos, monticelllo/Adobe Stock Photos.

Page 91: Dmitry Ersler/Adobe Stock Photos, C&OPhoto/Adobe Stock Photos, glebchik/Adobe Stock Photos, goir/Adobe Stock Photos, Coprid/Adobe Stock Photos, baibaz/Adobe Stock Photos.

Page 92: EastWest Imaging/Adobe Stock Photos, Eisenhans/Adobe Stock Photos, Andrey Popov/Adobe Stock Photos, Julie LEGRAND/Adobe Stock Photos, Ideenkoch/Adobe Stock Photos, 9nong/Adobe Stock Photos, LIGHTFIELD STUDIOS/Adobe Stock Photos, qech/Adobe Stock Photos, Jürgen Priewe/Adobe Stock Photos.

Chapter 05

Page 96: Jecapix/Getty Images, JaysonPhotography/Getty Images, ArtMarie/Getty Images, Aris Suwanmalee/Adobe Stock Photos, izusek/Getty Images, ChenPG/Adobe Stock Photos, ratana_k/Adobe Stock Photos.

Page 98: Marcus Lindstrom/Getty Images, FG Trade/Getty Images, Elenathewise/Adobe Stock Photos.

Page 99: Africa Studio/Adobe Stock Photos, Maygutyak/Adobe Stock Photos, nikkytok/Adobe Stock Photos.

Page 100: robepco/Adobe Stock Photos, Roman Babakin/Adobe Stock Photos, abramsdesign/Adobe Stock Photos, Viktoriya/Adobe Stock Photos, rootstocks/Adobe Stock Photos, pkanchana/Adobe Stock Photos, Carolyn Franks/Adobe Stock Photos, ekim/Adobe Stock Photos, Dmitry Naumov/Adobe Stock Photos, P&G/Adobe Stock Photos, LoloStock/Adobe Stock Photos, NorGal/Adobe Stock Photos.

Page 101: Myroslava/Adobe Stock Photos, arthito/Adobe Stock Photos.

Page 102: Christian Hillebrand/Adobe Stock Photos, bmak/Adobe Stock Photos, Photographee.eu/Adobe Stock Photos, Mongkolchon/Adobe Stock Photos, Monart Design/Adobe Stock Photos, Alex/Adobe Stock Photos, Patryk Kosmider/Adobe Stock Photos, karakedi35/Adobe Stock Photos, Owen/Adobe Stock Photos, Leigh Prather/Adobe Stock Photos, Sashkin/Adobe Stock Photos, karamysh/Adobe Stock Photos.

Page 103: Konstantin L/Adobe Stock Photos, zphoto83/Adobe Stock Photos, neirfy/Adobe Stock Photos, Cinematographer/Adobe Stock Photos, kichigin19/Adobe Stock Photos, didecs/Adobe Stock Photos, ThamKC/Adobe Stock Photos, Axel Bueckert/Adobe Stock Photos, SkyLine/Adobe Stock Photos.

Page 105: DGLimages/Getty Images, rilueda/Adobe Stock Photos, triocean/Adobe Stock Photos, Photographee.eu/Adobe Stock Photos, New Africa/Adobe Stock Photos, Rawf8/Adobe Stock Photos, manuta/Adobe Stock Photos, Pixel-Shot/Adobe Stock Photos.

Page 106: Svitlana/Adobe Stock Photos, Iriana Shiyan/Adobe Stock Photos, ezstudiophoto/Adobe Stock Photos, lisess/Adobe Stock Photos, olly/Adobe Stock Photos, Oleksandr Delyk/Adobe Stock Photos, pickup/Adobe Stock Photos, tiero/Adobe Stock Photos,

Herbivore/Adobe Stock Photos, Naypong Studio/Adobe Stock Photos, Kateryna/Adobe Stock Photos, timofeev/Adobe Stock Photos.

Page 107: Jacob Lund/Adobe Stock Photos, Kadmy/Adobe Stock Photos, rontech2000/Adobe Stock Photos, diy13/Adobe Stock Photos.

Page 108: poplasen/Adobe Stock Photos, Nomad_Soul/Adobe Stock Photos, New Africa/Adobe Stock Photos, ddukang/Adobe Stock Photos, Victor Moussa/Adobe Stock Photos, maykal/Adobe Stock Photos, goir/Adobe Stock Photos, bigacis/Adobe Stock Photos, Rostislav Sedlacek/Adobe Stock Photos, BillionPhotos.com/Adobe Stock Photos, Jackin/Adobe Stock Photos, DenisProduction.com/Adobe Stock Photos.

Page 109: Simone/Adobe Stock Photos, Olga Mishyna/Adobe Stock Photos, fotoduets/Adobe Stock Photos, TShum/Getty Images, Popova Olga/Adobe Stock Photos, alexnikit/Adobe Stock, chatchawan/Adobe Stock Photos, Ian 2010/Adobe Stock Photos, Mehmet Dilsiz/Adobe Stock Photos, Bits and Splits/Adobe Stock Photos, sebra/Adobe Stock, dred2010/Adobe Stock Photos.

Chapter 06

Page 112: alexlmx/Adobe Stock Photos, Vladimir Gerasimov/Adobe Stock Photos, alter_photo/Adobe Stock Photos, Kenishirotie/Adobe Stock Photos, darren415/Adobe Stock Photos, Julydfg/Adobe Stock Photos, chrisdorney/Adobe Stock Photos, svetlaborovko/Adobe Stock Photos.

Page 114: New Africa/Adobe Stock Photos, StudioStoltz/Adobe Stock Photos, VAKSMANV/Adobe Stock Photos, pxhere, Jacob Lund/Adobe Stock Photos, Jacob Lund/Adobe Stock Photos, industrieblick/Adobe Stock Photos, Addoro/Adobe Stock Photos, Addoro/Adobe Stock Photos, motortion/Adobe Stock Photos, Brian Jackson/Adobe Stock Photos.

Page 116: daniilvolkov/Adobe Stock Photos, amstockphoto/Adobe Stock Photos, Mat Hayward/Adobe Stock Photos, VAKSMANV/Adobe Stock Photos, Dario Lo Presti/Adobe Stock Photos, JackF/Getty Images, herraez/Adobe Stock Photos, Photoagriculture/Adobe Stock Photos, JackF/Adobe Stock Photos, JackF/Adobe Stock Photos, sergantstar/Adobe Stock Photos, KCULP/Adobe Stock Photos.

Page 117: Adrienne/Adobe Stock Photos, pbombaert/Adobe Stock Photos, LuckyPhoto/Adobe Stock Photos, zphoto83/Adobe Stock Photos, bigy9950/Adobe Stock Photos, arpatsara/Adobe Stock Photos, dmitrimaruta/Adobe Stock Photos, New Africa/Adobe Stock Photos.

Page 119: MicroOne/Adobe Stock Photos, mipan/Getty Images, fascinadora/Adobe Stock Photos, YesPhotographers/Adobe Stock Photos, xamtiw/Adobe Stock Photos, caftor/Adobe Stock Photos, Kondor83/Getty Images, Sharif_Whitebear/Adobe Stock Photos, adisa/Adobe Stock Photos, Image by Thomas B. from Pixabay, monticelllo/Adobe Stock Photos, Tyler Olson/Adobe Stock Photos.

Page 120: bignai/Adobe Stock Photos, WavebreakMediaMicro/Adobe Stock Photos, Maxim Grebeshkov/Adobe Stock Photos, Tyler Olson/Adobe Stock Photos.

Page 122: Photo by Julia Larson from Pexels, lexan/Adobe Stock Photos, Photo by Liza Summer from Pexels.

Page 123: nanjan/Adobe Stock Photos, Photo by Bruno Cantuária from Pexels, photology1971/Adobe Stock Photos, hal_pand_108/Adobe Stock Photos, kosolovskyy/Adobe Stock Photos, Image by efes from Pixabay, Tatiana/Adobe Stock Photos, JackF/Adobe Stock Photos, kojala/Adobe Stock Photos, Ivan Karpov/Adobe Stock Photos, kittima/Adobe Stock Photos, Светлана Соколова/Adobe Stock Photos.

Page 124: PIXELS, Monkey Business/Adobe Stock Photos, golubovy/Adobe Stock Photos, moodboard/Adobe Stock Photos, igishevamaria/Adobe Stock Photos.

Page 126: nito/Adobe Stock Photos, ksena32/Adobe Stock Photos, aimy27feb/Adobe Stock Photos, OBprod/Adobe Stock Photos, Restyler/Adobe Stock Photos, Evgeniya369/Adobe Stock Photos, Alexandra_K/Adobe Stock Photos, Tarzhanova/Adobe Stock Photos, mstudio/Adobe Stock Photos, Elena Stepanova/Adobe Stock Photos, Tarzhanova/Adobe Stock Photos, Valentin/Adobe Stock Photos.

Page 127: the_lightwriter/Adobe Stock Photos, Alexandra_K/Adobe Stock Photos, Olga/Adobe Stock Photos, Taeksang/Adobe Stock Photos, Khvost/Adobe Stock Photos, ViDi Studio/Adobe Stock Photos, eightstock/Adobe Stock Photos, srki66/Adobe Stock Photos, Un-Branded (P4MM)/Adobe Stock Photos, Monkey Business/Adobe Stock Photos, Елизавета Коробкова/Adobe Stock Photos.

Page 128: Ruggiero Scardigno/Adobe Stock Photos, sumire8/Adobe Stock Photos, Argus/Adobe Stock Photos, wabeno/Adobe Stock Photos, Dmitriy Syechin/Adobe Stock Photos, 01elena10/Adobe Stock Photos, pkleindienst/Adobe Stock Photos, Image by CNF Vector from Pixabay, Jitka Svetnickova/Adobe Stock Photos, Tierney/Adobe Stock Photos, Jacob Lund/Adobe Stock Photos, Spectral-Design/Adobe Stock Photos.

Page 129: gubh83/Adobe Stock Photos, gubh83/Adobe Stock Photos, gubh83/Adobe Stock Photos, gubh83/Adobe Stock Photos, gubh83/Adobe Stock Photos, Cobalt/Adobe Stock Photos, gubh83/Adobe Stock Photos, gubh83/Adobe Stock Photos, gubh83/Adobe Stock Photos, gubh83/Adobe Stock Photos, Cobalt/Adobe Stock Photos.

Page 131: Popova Olga/Adobe Stock Photos, nata777_7/Adobe Stock Photos, Dmitriy Golbay/Adobe Stock Photos, thithawat/Adobe Stock Photos, picsfive/Adobe Stock Photos, Valentina/Adobe Stock Photos, ksena32/Adobe Stock Photos, uwimages/Adobe Stock Photos, leungchopan/Adobe Stock Photos, New Africa/Adobe Stock Photos, Andrey Popov/Adobe Stock Photos, Alexandr Vlassyuk/Adobe Stock Photos.

Page 132: jackmac34/Pixabay, Valerii Zan/Adobe Stock Photos.

Page 133: gennadiy75/Adobe Stock Photos, MikeBiTa/Adobe Stock Photos, Tanya Rozhnovskaya/Adobe Stock Photos, Tiler84/Adobe Stock Photos, Pcess609/Adobe Stock Photos, peterschreiber.media/Adobe Stock Photos, photoblink/Adobe Stock Photos, Yakobchuk Olena/Adobe Stock Photos, cipariss/Adobe Stock Photos, sombats/Adobe Stock Photos, igorkol_ter/Adobe Stock Photos, yod77/Adobe Stock Photos.

Page 134: ETAP/Adobe Stock Photos, Kaspars Grinvalds/Adobe Stock Photos, Andrzej Tokarski/Adobe Stock Photos, foxdammit/Adobe Stock Photos, foxdammit/Adobe Stock Photos, katrin_timoff/Adobe Stock Photos, Nick Beer/Adobe Stock Photos, Vladimir Sazonov/Adobe Stock Photos, dechevm/Adobe Stock Photos, ket4up/Adobe Stock Photos.

Page 135: mumemories/Adobe Stock Photos, Marcin/Adobe Stock Photos, goldenangel/Adobe Stock Photos, westmarmaros/Adobe Stock Photos, zhukovvvlad/Adobe Stock Photos, A2LE/Adobe Stock Photos, Leonid Tit/Adobe Stock Photos, Lizzi 25/Adobe Stock Photos, Hans/Pixabay, Matthias/Adobe Stock Photos, Angelov/Adobe Stock Photos, Taken/Pixabay.

Page 136: Maridav/Adobe Stock Photos, Skitterphoto/Pexels, den-belitsky/Adobe Stock Photos, skeeze/Pixabay, yossarian6/Adobe Stock Photos, jc/Adobe Stock Photos, Elenathewise/Adobe Stock Photos, rangizzz/Adobe Stock Photos, Microgen/Adobe Stock Photos, VIAR PRO studio/Adobe Stock Photos, Tropical studio/Adobe Stock Photos, Pasko Maksim /Adobe Stock Photos.

Page 137: maewjpho/Adobe Stock Photos, pololia/Adobe Stock Photos, Gretchen Owen/Adobe Stock Photos, wavebreak3/Adobe Stock Photos, Marino Bocelli/Adobe Stock Photos, mirkomedia/Adobe Stock Photos, WavebreakMediaMicro/Adobe Stock Photos, Shane/Adobe Stock Photos, sportpoint/Adobe Stock Photos, NDABCREATIVITY/Adobe Stock Photos, blueiz60/Adobe Stock Photos, Maridav/Adobe Stock Photos.

Page 138: Karen Arehart/Adobe Stock Photos, Akaberka/Adobe Stock Photos.

Page 139: BestForYou/Adobe Stock Photos, Dusan Kostic/Adobe Stock Photos, primipil/Adobe Stock Photos, KeithJJ/Pixabay, vectorfusionart/Adobe Stock Photos, inproperstyle/Pixabay, _italo_/Adobe Stock Photos, WavebreakMediaMicro/Adobe Stock Photos, fotofabrika/Adobe Stock Photos.

Page 140: CJ Cauley/Pexels, Fineart Panorama/Adobe Stock Photos, srongkrod/Adobe Stock Photos, hy-studio/Adobe Stock Photos, danny tu/Shutterstock, Michael Evans/Adobe Stock Photos, stockbp/Adobe Stock Photos, fotoplaton/Adobe Stock Photos, Alexandra_K/Adobe Stock Photos, stux/Pixabay, Ingus Evertovskis/Adobe Stock Photos, cammep/Adobe Stock Photos.

Page 141: jakkapan/Adobe Stock Photos, bennnn/Adobe Stock Photos, timonko/Adobe Stock Photos, boophotography/Adobe Stock Photos, Evgeny Korshenkov/Adobe Stock Photos, Rachanon/Adobe Stock Photos, dcorneli/Adobe Stock Photos, snaptitude/Adobe Stock Photos, AnnaMoskvina/Adobe Stock Photos, haveseen/Adobe Stock Photos, Africa Studio/Adobe Stock Photos, Films42/Pixabay.

Page 142: Rostislav Ageev/Adobe Stock Photos, photomelon/Adobe Stock Photos, texturewall/Adobe Stock Photos, nndanko/Adobe Stock Photos, itsallgood/Adobe Stock Photos, Sonja/Adobe Stock Photos, IrkIngwer/Adobe Stock Photos, Ariwasabi/Adobe Stock Photos, Fredy Thürig/Adobe Stock Photos, dimitrisvetsikas1969/Pixabay.

Page 144: Elenathewise/Adobe Stock Photos, summa/Pixabay, Ta-niaVdB/Pixabay, THP Creative/Adobe Stock Photos, topshots/Adobe Stock Photos, Bondarau/Adobe Stock Photos, nata_rass/Adobe Stock Photos, eshana_blue/Adobe Stock Photos.

Page 146: auremar/Adobe Stock Photos, IvicaNS/Adobe Stock Photos, gnepphoto/Adobe Stock Photos, AntonioDiaz/Adobe Stock Photos, Gowtham/Adobe Stock Photos, Mark Poprocki/Adobe Stock Photos, nicoletaionescu/Adobe Stock Photos.

Page 148: LiliWhite/Adobe Stock Photos, ZoneCreative/Adobe Stock Photos, Yay Images/Adobe Stock Photos, Mangostar/Adobe Stock Photos, bruno135_406/Adobe Stock Photos, Anton Gvozdikov/Adobe Stock Photos.

Page 149: Gary/Adobe Stock Photos, wikimedia commons, Jan Rose/Adobe Stock Photos, Pavel Losevsky/Adobe Stock Photos, kozlik_mozlik/Adobe Stock Photos, VIAR PRO studio/Adobe Stock Photos, master1305/Adobe Stock Photos, Orlando Florin Rosu/Adobe Stock Photos, Ivan Hafizov/Adobe Stock Photos, kozlik_mozlik/Adobe Stock Photos, kozlik_mozlik/Adobe Stock Photos.

Page 151: Travel_Master/Adobe Stock Photos, serikbaib/Adobe Stock Photos, Pavel Losevsky/Adobe Stock Photos, Vladimir Wrangel/Adobe Stock Photos, 4th Life Photography/Adobe Stock Photos, LUMEZIA.com/Adobe Stock Photos, FrankBoston/Adobe Stock Photos, Serjio/Adobe Stock Photos.

Page 153: Africa Studio/Adobe Stock Photos, sforzza/Adobe Stock Photos, deagreez/Adobe Stock Photos, алексей балтенков/Adobe Stock Photos, master1305/Adobe Stock Photos, xy/Adobe Stock Photos, pongsakorn_jun26/Adobe Stock Photos, Pixabay, moodboard/Adobe Stock Photos, One/Adobe Stock Photos, Glenda Powers/Adobe Stock Photos, frank peters/Adobe Stock Photos.

Page 154: Pexels, Nikolai Sorokin/Adobe Stock Photos, AGCuesta/Adobe Stock Photos, James Steidl/Adobe Stock Photos, vetkit/Adobe Stock Photos, Africa Studio/Adobe Stock Photos.

Chapter 07

Page 158: Rido/Adobe Stock Photos, LoloStock/Adobe Stock Photos, razoomanetu/Adobe Stock Photos, vladimirfloyd/Adobe Stock Photos, littlestocker/Adobe Stock Photos, Krakenimages.com/Adobe Stock Photos, filistimlyanin1/Adobe Stock Photos,

Alex/Adobe Stock Photos, Zemler/Adobe Stock Photos, mraoraor/Adobe Stock Photos, Microgen/Adobe Stock Photos, exzozis/Adobe Stock Photos.

Page 159: javiindy/Adobe Stock Photos, yellowj/Adobe Stock Photos, mraoraor/Adobe Stock Photos, WavebreakMediaMicro/Adobe Stock Photos, Glebstock/Adobe Stock Photos, vladimirfloyd/Adobe Stock Photos, Axel Kock/Adobe Stock Photos, Anatomy Insider/Adobe Stock Photos, alexlmx/Adobe Stock Photos, Bohdan/Adobe Stock Photos, Maksym Yemelyanov/Adobe Stock Photos, adimas/Adobe Stock Photos.

Page 160: eranicle/Adobe Stock Photos, rommma/Adobe Stock Photos, SciePro/Adobe Stock Photos.

Page 162: Syda Productions/Adobe Stock Photos, kei907/Adobe Stock Photos, AlenKadr/Adobe Stock Photos, narongchaihlaw/Adobe Stock Photos, Liudmila Dutko/Adobe Stock Photos, rufar/Adobe Stock Photos, blackday/Adobe Stock Photos, Kurhan/Adobe Stock Photos, schankz/Adobe Stock Photos, ninell/Adobe Stock Photos, PixieMe/Adobe Stock Photos, Aleksandr Rybalko/Adobe Stock Photos.

Page 163: booleen/Adobe Stock Photos, Евгений Вдовин/Adobe Stock Photos, elavuk81/Adobe Stock Photos, Johanna Goodyear/Adobe Stock Photos, Chris Tefme/Adobe Stock Photos, vladimirfloyd/Adobe Stock Photos.

Page 164: Simone van den Berg/Adobe Stock Photos, bnenin/Adobe Stock Photos, rh2010/Adobe Stock Photos, Africa Studio/Adobe Stock Photos, romaset/Adobe Stock Photos, Syda Productions/Adobe Stock Photos, zeremskimilan/Adobe Stock Photos, WavebreakMediaMicro/Adobe Stock Photos, Minerva Studio/Adobe Stock Photos, rogerphoto/Adobe Stock Photos.

Page 166: emiliau/Adobe Stock Photos, Piman Khrutmuang/Adobe Stock Photos, John Neff/Adobe Stock Photos, Davizro Photography/Adobe Stock Photos, rainbow33/Adobe Stock Photos, metamorworks/Adobe Stock Photos, Andrey Popov/Adobe Stock Photos, gallofilm/Adobe Stock Photos, Sven Vietense/Adobe Stock Photos, sebra/Adobe Stock Photos, tugolukof/Adobe Stock Photos, zinkevych/Adobe Stock Photos.

Page 167: RFBSIP/Adobe Stock Photos, sebra/Adobe Stock Photos, Andrey Popov/Adobe Stock Photos, Oksana_S/Adobe Stock Photos, decade3d/Adobe Stock Photos, BillionPhotos.com/Adobe Stock

Photos, piXuLariUm/Adobe Stock Photos, gopfaster/Adobe Stock Photos, lavizzara/Adobe Stock Photos, Ольга Тернавская/Adobe Stock Photos, Kaspars Grinvalds/Adobe Stock Photos.

Page 169: Tyler Olson/Adobe Stock Photos, sebra/Adobe Stock Photos, photophonie/Adobe Stock Photos, BestForYou/Adobe Stock Photos, James Thew/Adobe Stock Photos, Dario Lo Presti/Adobe Stock Photos, SKatzenberger/Adobe Stock Photos, tuulijumala/Adobe Stock Photos, Sly/Adobe Stock Photos, 18percentgrey/Adobe Stock Photos, Graphicroyalty/Adobe Stock Photos, Burlingham/Adobe Stock Photos.

Page 170: Юлия Пипкина/Adobe Stock Photos, photolink/Adobe Stock Photos, Paylessimages/Adobe Stock Photos, gna60/Adobe Stock Photos, blackday/Adobe Stock Photos, Andrzej Wilusz/Adobe Stock Photos.

Page 172: itsallgood/Adobe Stock Photos, PhotoEdit/Adobe Stock Photos, Sheri Armstrong/Adobe Stock Photos, adragan/Adobe Stock Photos, Kurhan/Adobe Stock Photos, rocketclips/Adobe Stock Photos.

Page 174: Andrey Popov/Adobe Stock Photos, Ruzanna/Adobe Stock Photos, magdal3na/Adobe Stock Photos, Rawpixel.com/Adobe Stock Photos, spyross007/Adobe Stock Photos, tippapatt/Adobe Stock Photos, Herbivore/Adobe Stock Photos, hedgehog94/Adobe Stock Photos.